OUT *of the* DARKNESS

THE FAIELLA FAMILY'S JOURNEY TO RECOVER THEIR AUTISTIC SON

Foreword by J.B Handley,
Co-founder of Generation Rescue

DANIEL FAIELLA

Special Thanks

Thanks to all medical professionals and caregivers attempting to help children afflicted with this condition, which through their unfaltering determination have shown that there is hope.

For everyone suffering from this misunderstood and often misdiagnosed disorder and their families / caregivers that must walk this road with them.

Daniel Faiella

Author Note

Every individual's body chemistry is unique to that individual. The treatment results described in this book are not guaranteed to be the best course to follow for everyone and those seeking assistance should consider all possible side-effects of each before proceeding with any. The procedures and therapies discussed in this book are by all means not the only methods of treatment available. Please research any and all possible avenues as well as consulting with your own medical practitioner(s) to determine the best course of action for your particular issue before taking action. The writers of this book are not responsible for any injuries incurred as a result of following the treatments herein. The opinions regarding all medical practices and procedures are those of the writers alone. No one should base their decisions to follow or not follow any course of treatment based solely on these opinions and the writers are not libel for any injuries should they occur from following these opinions.

Everyday of life is a journey. Join us on ours.

Table of Contents

GodSpeed

Lyrics by Victoria Faiella

Music by Barry Hartglass
and Victoria Faiella

Available at
http://www.victoriafaiella.com

Do you know how much you're loved?
More than all the Stars
More than words can explain
An eternity of telling you
Would prove to be in vain

I thought I understood Love
Absolute and True
Until fate brought me You

Out of the Darkness

If our last hope
Hangs on a wire
Do anything I can
I'll walk through the fire
No mountains' too high
No valley too deep
To save my precious child
Wish me Godspeed

Do you know how much you're loved?
More than life itself
More than words can express
An eternity of telling you
Would be wasted breath

Do you know that you'll be loved
Till the end of Time
Love like this never dies

Dedicated to and written for our son, Matthew.

Foreword

What would you do?
Your child, developing normally, starts to change. Subtly at first, and then more extreme. Your doubts grow, and so do your fears. Before you know it, the child you once knew is gone. After many painful visits to doctors, clinicians, diagnosticians, you finally get the word: autism.

Along with the diagnosis, you're also told how hopeless things may be for your child: no independent living, no marriage, no friends, and perhaps no words. An institution beckons down the road. Get 'em into ABA (Applied Behavior Analysis) you're told, and hope for the best. Sorry, this must be so hard for you. That's it.

For a moment, your whole world stops, you're overcome by grief and despair. With what little energy you have, you start to read and learn. Some of the things you are reading seem crazy after what you've been told: kids are recovering? Vaccines may be involved? Special diets? Chelation? B-12? HBOT?

You feel overwhelmed. Behind one door, you have the mainstream, telling you things are nearly hopeless. But, behind this door #2, in a world you never knew existed, things sound a hell of a lot better.

What would you do?
Would you fold your tent and do what the doctors told you, or would you join the parents of recovered kids and fight like hell to make your child the next great recovery story?

I know what Daniel Faiella did, he chose door #2, he chose to fight for his son. In doing so, he has blazed a path for others to follow. Is stem cell therapy the answer for all children with autism? I don't know. What we do know is that it's helping our kids recover from something we've been told is life long and permanent. Every door should be opened, every path should be considered to help our kids, and Daniel's journey with his own son is instructive for other families trying to figure out how to help their child.

Autism is reversible, recovery is real. Just ask Daniel Faiella – I'm grateful he chose to share his story with you.

JB Handley
Generation Rescue

I Want to Talk to Papa

The same thought that entered Ruth's mind on the ride out silently crept back to the forefront as she drove home from the doctor's office. How was she going to make this trip every day for the next two weeks? Two hours to Melbourne, treatment for two hours then two hours back for something that seemed hopeless. She checked on her son Matthew sitting in his booster seat in the middle of the backseat. He looked okay as he watched the portable DVD player Ruth had brought to keep him occupied during the long drive.

Both she and her husband Daniel had exhausted themselves researching hyperbaric oxygen therapy. Some clinical trials of its use with autistic patients had been documented however, it had yet to be fully FDA approved as a viable form of treatment for the disorder. In fact, many doctors strongly opposed the therapy.

If it did work, how could she and Daniel afford it? Insurance wouldn't pay a cent, using the medical community's doubts and misconceptions as their excuse. With the cost so astronomical, the next two weeks of treatments were all they could currently afford. The price of each treatment came directly out of their pocket. Doing any more would place them dangerously in debt. Buying a chamber for home use was mind-numbing. The starting price was twenty thousand dollars.

Ruth didn't have high hopes of seeing any improvement in their son's condition after his two weeks of treatment were completed. The doctor had been careful to warn them not to expect too much. He mentioned the majority of children usually don't show any type of improvement whatsoever until sometime after their fortieth treatment. Still, Ruth and Daniel had decided that they would give it a try and see what happened.

Her ringing cell phone drowned out her thoughts bringing her back to the moment. She pulled it out and checked the number. It was Daniel calling from work during his break.

"Hey."

"How did it go?"

1

Before Ruth could respond she heard her son speak from his seat in the back.

"Is that Papa? I want to talk to Papa."

Ruth's throat closed up. She tried to speak but couldn't. Tears formed in the corners of her eyes, blurring her vision. She pulled over to the shoulder and cried as she turned in her chair to look at her son. At six years old, it was the first time he had spoken more than two words together. It was at that moment that she decided both her and her husband would have to find a way to somehow continue with the treatments.

Family

Family had always been important to Ruth. Born in Lockport, New York, she couldn't recall much of her time there since her father had decided to move the family to West Virginia after her eighth birthday. This was mainly due to economic reasons. Being the baby of five sisters and two brothers, there was always a sense of unity and strength within her family. All the siblings were close, with the older ones constantly looking out for their younger brothers and sisters.

Ruth didn't know how much that strength would be tested until her older sister Maycle, still living in New York, began getting sick. Her mild symptoms progressed into much more disturbing signs such as bleeding from her gums, sudden extreme weakness in her arms and legs, rapid weight loss as well as bruising and bone pain. After she was put through many tests, the kids were told their sister had leukemia. She was put on an aggressive chemotherapy schedule and became very frail. Ruth's mother would drive back into the city to take care of her for weeks at a time.

Ruth was very young but had to grow up fast as the reality of what was happening to her sister took hold. All of the things she thought were important up to that point faded away as her family tried to figure out how best to help her sister recover.

Maycle struggled in pain for several years before finally succumbing to her illness. Ruth's sister was finally laid to rest on what began as a pleasant, sunny summer day in April of 1987. As the preacher began the eulogy, the sky darkened and rain began falling. Ruth, ten years old, was numb as she looked around at the dozens of people that had come to pay their respects to her sister in the packed cemetery. There were so many people that the parked cars trailed out of the cemetery gates and onto the service road outside. Maycle was twenty-two years old.

After the initial shock of their loss wore off, the search for answers as to why Maycle was taken from them so young began to drive Ruth's family. They would discover that her grandfather on her mother's side had passed away in the same agonizing way, from the same horrible disease. Astonishingly, he was only thirty years old when he died.

Out of the Darkness

She and her family did what most family's do in the face of this type of situation; they grieved then picked up their lives as best they could and began living again, one day at a time. She couldn't have known then that cancer would touch her again so profoundly or so soon.

Meeting in Florida

Ruth decided to move to Florida in 1995, partly to get on with the business of living. She stayed with her sister Pauline who had already left home, moving to the state a few years earlier. Her decision would eventually lead her to meet the man she would fall in love with and marry.

Daniel was born in Bronx, New York. He was also the baby in his family, having ten older brothers and sisters. Although born a New Yorker, Daniel considered himself a Floridian, spending much of his childhood growing up in the Sunshine State. He too had left New York while still young and didn't recall many memories of it. His family had grown tired of life in the hectic city and really enjoyed the climate and culture of the south, remembering it fondly from past vacations. He was five years old when his parents decided to move his family to Kissimmee, Florida.

Aside from a larger than average family, Daniel had a relatively normal childhood. At eight years old, he began to experience a reoccurring dream that would follow him for the rest of his adolescent life. The dream was always the same and in it he was a grown man with a son of his own. Even at eight years old, he could tell his child had mental difficulties in the dream. His son was slow and unresponsive to those around him.

It bothered him whenever he thought about it during his waking hours. Daniel kept the dream to himself, not wanting anyone to know. In retrospect, he would often wonder what brought the dream about but could not find any trigger for it. No one, either in his family nor any friends that he knew, had dealt with such issues.

Later, Daniel's parents moved the family to Clearwater, Florida. It was there, while working at a telemarketing company, that he met Ruth. They went on their first of several dates on April 21, 1996. As time went on, their discussions began turning toward marriage. His dream had disturbed him so much over the years that he told Ruth he did not want to have children for fear of it coming true.

Out of the Darkness

She listened intently and agreed with him that they didn't have to have children. They loved each other and that was enough for her. They were married April 21, 1999, on a bright, sunny day with a small, family ceremony at a local city park. They had committed their lives to each other for better or worse and were thrilled. The whole world lay before them.

God's Will

Since both of them had agreed not to have children, Ruth proactively took contraception to ensure she would not conceive. Weeks after treating a severe ear infection with antibiotics, she felt different.

She couldn't explain how she knew, but felt that she was now pregnant. Ruth finally went out and bought a home pregnancy kit. She was shocked when it tested positive. Unknown to her at the time was that the antibiotic she had taken to heal her ear could, in some instances, affect the potency of the contraceptive medication she was on. Taking both at the same time could negate or weaken the effects of the pill. After their initial surprise, both her and Daniel were ecstatic with their turn of events and decided that God had intervened. They were going to have a baby and nothing was going to stop it.

Matthew was born, by cesarean, on November 22, 2000, at 11:43 in the evening. Their son was put through the standard checks, cleaned, bundled up and handed over to them. The doctor and nurses declared Matthew healthy and congratulated the proud new parents. Ruth smiled and then told Daniel he didn't have to worry, that his dream was untrue. Daniel breathed a sigh of relief as a big weight was lifted off his shoulders. He put the fear out of his mind. They had a healthy child and brought Matthew home, eager to begin their new life together.

Daniel and Matthew say hello to each other for the first time.

Milestones

Even though everything seemed fine, Daniel couldn't shake the thought that his dream might still come to fruition. Since Matthew's birth, it had always lingered in the back of his mind, refusing to let go of him completely. This was one of the reasons why he and Ruth were hesitant to administer vaccinations. By this time, they had heard on the news about therimosol possibly causing autism and discovered it present in not only the RH shot that Ruth had received just past the half-way mark in her pregnancy, but in many common childhood vaccines as well.

Their family pediatrician strongly urged them to reconsider. When that didn't work, the tactics changed. She would refuse to treat their son unless they agreed to vaccination shots. Daniel and Ruth were also told that their son wouldn't be allowed into school and that they wouldn't be able to find a pediatrician willing to add them to their patient rosters.

Daniel would say later, "Everyone made us feel like bad parents when all we wanted to do was protect our child. We had learned of what was in the RH shot after the fact and just wanted the best for our boy."

Daniel and Ruth scrambled to locate someone to take care of their son while they both worked. His daycare informed them that he would not be able to stay at their facility unless vaccinated. Unsuccessful and continually being pressured to vaccinate, they finally relented.

They stressed mercury-free vaccines be administered and had their doctor check the lot numbers of the vials used on their son. They didn't know at the time that even vaccines labeled therimosol-free could potentially include up to ten percent of the toxin nor did they realize that although levels of therimosol had been drastically reduced, it had been replaced with aluminum, another toxic metal.[1]

Daniel's fears subsided when Matthew met all of his early projected milestones on or before the average time. He was consistently in the ninety to ninety-five percentiles on height and weight at every checkup

---

[1] For a complete listing of vaccine ingredients, point your web browser to http://www.novaccine.com/vaccine-ingredients/

and appeared healthy. Matthew's personality, at six months old, was happy and affectionate.

He loved to play with his parents and ate very well. Daniel noticed that his son never really cried and was usually content to play by himself rather than interacting with friends and family. He eventually began to say single words at eleven months and it was around this same time that he began walking.

The 'C' Word

The early part of 2001 was a very good time for the Faiella family. Daniel and Ruth were happily married and enjoying their new son who by all accounts appeared to be thriving. The thoughts of Daniel's childhood dreams faded as the months filtered by. That would change suddenly in May of that same year.

One morning, Ruth walked out of the bedroom with a look of concern across her face. She hesitated slightly before telling Daniel she had felt a lump during her monthly breast examination. As soon as she could, Ruth contacted her doctor and set up an appointment to get it examined.

At her appointment, Ruth's Gynecologist told her she shouldn't worry. He mentioned that because of her age, twenty-five years old, and the fact that it didn't run in her family, she was not a likely candidate for breast cancer. He told her she should focus on her child and husband and not worry about it.

In the meantime, just to quell their doubts, he would arrange an ultrasound in order to make sure everything was okay. Daniel and Ruth waited anxiously for the results. The test had said she was negative for cancer. Their fears subsided but only slightly.

Six months later, Ruth felt the lump again. It seemed larger to her. After telling Daniel, they decided that this time they needed to talk to another doctor instead. That doctor, a general practitioner, told them Ruth had done everything right statistically in order to not get breast cancer.

The meeting was basically the same as the one they had undergone six months earlier with her gynecologist. She speculated that Ruth had developed a common cyst due to glucose build-up from drinking too much soda. She did however, suggest Ruth have a mammogram as a precautionary measure. It would allow a better picture, through the use of low-dose x-rays, to show them what, if anything, was going on.

Neither Ruth nor Daniel was prepared for the results of the test. It showed a three centimeter growth easily identified in Ruth's left breast. They were referred to a surgeon who followed up the test with a needle-nose biopsy as quickly as possible to confirm.

They sat in the office, as Matthew played in his mother's lap, while the doctor relayed his findings from Ruth's follow-up. There was no denying it. The tests had shown a very large and very aggressive, estrogen-negative, HER2-positive malignant tumor.

Estrogen-negative meant that the cancer cells did not contain estrogen receptors and therefore did not require estrogen to grow as many breast cancers do. Since tamoxifen, the most prescribed successful breast cancer treating drug, utilizes anti-estrogen therapy in its treatment protocol this drug would be utterly useless to her. [2i] The doctor would have to use alternative drugs instead.

HER2, short for Human Epidermal growth factor Receptor 2, is a naturally occurring protein that regulates cell growth and reproduction. HER2-positive meant a large amount of this protein was flooding Ruth's system and, in turn, causing an excessive amount of growth and reproduction of cancer cells as well. [3ii] The cells were dividing at a very alarming rate and had been since the beginning.

They speculated with the doctor as to how long the tumor had been growing since it was so large. They concluded that it had begun while Ruth was still in her teens. Now that it had been discovered that something was wrong, the next hurdle to tackle was what to do about it.

Ruth was told that the growth should be removed as soon as possible and that taking it out was no guarantee that it wouldn't come back. She asked where it might come back and the doctor mentioned her other breast. Not wanting to take a chance and have to go through the process a second time, Ruth instructed him to take both breasts agreeing to have a double mastectomy.

During the operation, dye was injected into Ruth's lymph glands so the doctor could see how far the cancer had actually spread. It was worse than he initially thought. Ten of the lymph nodes in her chest and arm contained the cancer and needed removal immediately. The growth itself was nine centimeters instead of three. The doctor removed all affected lymph nodes as well has both of Ruth's breasts while she was under.

After removing the cancer, doctors began the process of inserting tissue expanders into Ruth's chest in preparation for reconstructive surgery. Expanders consist of inflatable balloon type apparatus implanted under the

2   Learn more at http://www.cancer.gov/cancertopics/factsheet/therapy/tamoxifen
3   Learn more about HER2 at http://www.gene.com/gene/products/education/oncology/her2disease.html

skin and injected with saline solution over an extended period of time. This slow and painful process forces the body to gradually grow additional skin, bone or other tissues.

A portacath, or port for short, was inserted into a large vein in Ruth's chest. This would allow easier administration of drugs and fluid removal during the planned chemotherapy treatments that were to follow. All would not go as planned.

While she was in recovery from the surgery, her body began rejecting the tissue expanders almost immediately and she started getting painful infections in the areas they had been inserted into. Even though her body constantly ached, the doctors opted to leave the expanders in for the time being. She would make many trips to the hospital over the next months fighting painful infections.

Ruth was categorized with late Stage IIIB cancer. Breast cancer is measured on a scale. The levels are Stage I, Stage II, Stage IIIA, Stage IIIB and Stage IV. Stage IIIB signifies that cancer has either spread from the breast to the surrounding tissues or it has infiltrated one or more of the body's lymph nodes. Ruth's lymphatic system, the body's primary defensive mechanism against infection, had been compromised. The lymph nodes, located just inside Ruth's chest wall and arm, were filled with cancer.

The only stage above hers, Stage IV, is characterized by cancer cells having spread to other regions and organs of the body. At late Stage IIIB, she was on the cusp of the fourth and final stage of the scale. Trying to be as optimistic as possible, the surgeon gave Ruth only a thirty percent chance of living longer than ten years.

Ruth decided to undergo gene testing to determine if the particular cancer afflicting her was genetic and could be passed within her family. She didn't want any of her loved ones caught off-guard like she had been. When the tests came back, she was relieved to discover that she had been the first in her family line for this particular type of cancer.

After her excruciating recovery from the surgery, Ruth was discharged from the hospital, and immediately began a heavy chemotherapy regime to make sure the cancer had been eradicated.

Chemotherapy required Daniel driving Ruth to the doctor's office once a month. She would receive her treatment from an intravenous drip through the port in her chest over a three hour period. He and Matthew would then drive back, pick her up, and take her home since she would not be able to drive herself. She would experience unbelievable pain both physically and mentally for the entire nine months of her treatments.

Following each session, without fail, she would lay in bed sometimes for days, not able to get up even to walk to other parts of the house. There were several times that she would refuse to eat or drink because her body felt so bad. Daniel had to tell her sternly more than a few times that he would drive her to the hospital for fluids if she didn't eat something. He would bring her fruit and wait for her to eat it, not leaving her side until he was sure she had done so.

As her treatments progressed over the next few months, all her hair fell out and she began to experience severe anxiety, spiking into random panic attacks for no known reason. Her sister Pauline moved in with the family and helped care for Matthew.

Both Ruth and Daniel tried to keep what was happening from the eyes of their son as best they could. They would discover that even at an early age, Matthew could comprehend something wasn't quite right. He would frequently stop playing quietly in the corner of the room to come over to his mother, who was lying on the couch. He would kiss her cheek gently and stroke her face before going back to his toys.

Ruth constantly worried about him not receiving enough attention from her. She would suddenly leave him, being admitted for infections and complications due to her treatments. Matthew would sit by her bedside staring at all the tubes snaking out of her weakened body and all the large, loud machines she was attached to. She wondered what her tiny boy was thinking each time he saw her like that.

A Change for the Worse

When Matthew turned fourteen months old, his father took him in for his scheduled first year evaluation. Ruth was in the hospital for a four day stay receiving antibiotics for an infection. She would get them off and on over the months due to the tissue expanders in her chest. The doctors tried to determine if she had MRSA, a highly infectious and resistant form of the Staphylococcus aureus bacterium, and she was not allowed to have visitors.

According to the pediatrician, everything checked out fine. Matthew's height and weight, though at the high end of the scale, were in line for his age. His motor skills and mental development seemed to be right on track.

During his first year, Matthew always smiled.

One of the last items of business during his visit was receiving a chicken pox vaccination. Daniel had slight reservations. He was told that Matthew could die if he got chicken pox unnecessarily. This scared Daniel and he allowed the pediatrician to give the shot to his son.

Two days after that doctor visit, he noticed something a little odd with Matthew. Even though his son hadn't displayed any of the normal warning signs of a reaction to the shot such as fussiness, vomiting, seizures or non-stop crying, he did seem to have withdrawn somewhat.

When Ruth came home from her hospital stay, she was upset with Matthew's reaction, or lack of one, toward her. He didn't reach out and say "up, momma". He simply continued to play by himself. For the last three months, any time she came home, he would always greet her with a big hug and kiss. Feeling horrible, she thought her son had forgotten her because she had been gone for four days. Even though she had made many trips to the hospital up to now, this was the first time she had stayed longer than a day.

Over the next few months, Matthew's behavior would continue to change. The words he had begun speaking before were slowly being re-placed with silence and he visibly became much more introverted. Easy puzzles that he had enjoyed putting together just weeks before now lay on the floor in a mess. He was unable to do them anymore. He wouldn't go to his parents any longer, or his Aunt Pauline. Instead of interacting with his family as he was so eager to do before, he closed himself off. They felt he was shutting them out but didn't know why.

His eating habits changed. His once excellent appetite shrank until it consisted of mainly milk and crispy bacon. Concerned, Ruth tried any-thing she could think of to get him to eat better but the result was always the same. He would turn away when food was offered, clamp his teeth tight and run away from the table. His doctor instructed Ruth to remove bacon from his diet entirely and he would have no choice but to eat what she provided. He refused to eat and after an agonizing two days, Ruth relented. She wasn't going to starve her son.

Ruth spoke to Matthew's pediatrician several times concerning all the changes she had seen. Each time the doctor reassured her that Matthew was fine and she had nothing to worry about.

What About Vaccines

Daniel and Ruth continued to have Matthew's pediatrician administer his vaccinations even after noticing him withdrawing. They had been ridiculed before for even hinting at considering postponing any vaccinations.

Since the beginning, they had been led to believe that their son would not be able to attend school going forward unless he received the full vaccination schedule on time. Even though they desperately wanted to discover what was happening to their son, they eventually succumbed to the pressure of the doctors.

About a year later, after researching more on their own, they found out that they could have applied for a personal beliefs waiver from the county they resided in. They would have had to sign a notarized document at their county health department. This would have allowed their son to continue attending daycare without receiving any vaccination shots or booster supplements. This fact had never been mentioned to them during any of their numerous doctor office or hospital visits.

Daniel's research into it had also uncovered possibly unethical practices and poisonous ingredients within certain vaccines. This led them to question whether or not the rigid and demanding immunization schedules had been in their son's best interest. It seemed the schedules were geared more toward the interests of the pharmaceutical companies supplying the vaccines.

Vaccines in the United States have grown into a large business in the last thirty years. The recommended number of vaccinations children receive has jumped from ten, in the early 1980's, to thirty-six in 2008. Many top pharmaceutical companies have paid substantially large sums of money to organizations such as The American Academy of Pediatrics and Every Child by Two. This support from pharmaceutical companies brings into question conflicts of interest within the organizations that are supposed to be protecting the children. [4iii]

---

4   To read more about the ethics of vaccines go to http://www.cbsnews.com/stories/2008/07/25/cbsnews_investigates/main4296175.shtml

Daniel would also research many facts leading him to doubt the additives in vaccines such as DTaP were even necessary and potentially hazardous, additives such as therimosol and aluminum. [5] Ingredients, whose seemingly only purpose for inclusion was to kill any bacteria in multi-dose vials. These toxic additives would not be necessary if the pharmaceutical companies were to distribute single-dose vials instead. This is not as cost-effective however.

Not only was the hazardous metals a factor but some of the vaccines contained live viruses as well. They would later hear, time and again, from many parents of similar changes in behavior of their own children after vaccination shots. Many had noticed subtle changes within days of vaccination and then a gradual decline in their children.

---

[5] To see a list of vaccine additives go to http://www.windsorpeak.com/baby411/additives.pdf

Something's Not Right

Since Daniel's family was larger and spread out across several states, it wasn't very often that he and his siblings could all get together at once. He was very eager when his older sister invited him to her house for a barbeque. She had made arrangements for almost all of their brothers and sisters to be there. It would be the first real reunion since they all left home over ten years ago. Many of his siblings' families would get to meet his now eighteen month old son. He wanted Matthew to have a good time with his cousins and Daniel wanted to catch up with everyone as well.

When the day finally arrived, Ruth wasn't feeling well enough to make the two hour drive to Daniel's sister's house. The chemotherapy she had to endure continued to make her sick. She told him to go ahead and take Matthew since Daniel was looking forward to going. She didn't want her pain to ruin it for him. Daniel told her to call him if she needed to, secured Matthew in his car seat, and began the long drive to the west coast of Florida.

At the barbeque, while Daniel chatted with his siblings, Matthew's ten cousins played games throughout the house. The kids ranged in age from their early teens down to little over a year. Daniel kept an eye on his son. He had grown a little concerned that Matthew had been playing in the corner by himself since they had arrived even though he had been introduced to his cousins. This was the first real time his son had been able to interact with several other kids around his own age and Daniel was eager to see how he would handle it.

Daniel's brother Stephen entered the house and Daniel greeted him at the front door. A gust of wind caught the door after Stephen entered, slamming it shut with a loud and sudden bang. Everyone in the room jumped, except Matthew who was sitting closest to the door playing. His head was still down, looking over the blocks he had been stacking quietly. Daniel immediately noticed Matthew's lack of shock and asked if anyone else had witnessed his son's reaction.

Stephen knelt down next to Matthew, snapping his fingers near his nephew's left ear. The boy continued playing, staring down at the blocks.

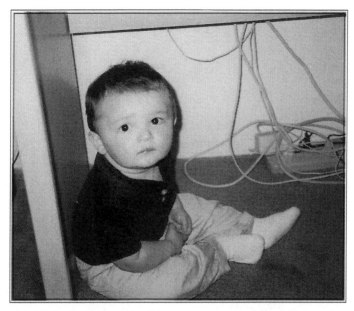

Matthew's ever present smile fades away.

Moving to his son's other side Daniel snapped his fingers close to Matthew's right ear, achieving the same result. Oh no, he's deaf, Daniel thought as he hit the auto dial on his cell phone to call Ruth at home.

Ruth told Daniel not to worry. She knew there was nothing they could do at the moment and that worrying Daniel would just ruin the rest of his visit. She calmed him and told him they would talk about it when he and Matthew returned home. Daniel could show her what he had seen and they could go from there.

As strong as she was for Daniel's sake, a part of her knew her son wasn't deaf. This realization sent a wave of fear though her entire body. She mentally recalled countless times in the past where she had been out of his line of sight, called his name low, and he had come running to her. As bad as it seemed for her to entertain the notion, a part of her secretly hoped he was deaf. If he wasn't, she knew something much worse was going on with him. After making sure Daniel was calm, Ruth said her goodbye's, hung up the phone and cried quietly.

Your Son Is Not Autistic

Matthew's parents set up an appointment with his pediatrician as quickly as possible, to voice their concerns and gather advice. The doctor listened to them then decided to have Matthew take a hearing test to rule out deafness. It was no surprise to Ruth when it came back negative. They were instructed to observe Matthew closely. It was likely he was just going through a phase. No other solutions were offered to them.

Based on the behaviors Ruth was witnessing, she and Daniel felt something else was going on. Over the course of a few months, they continued to demand something be done. They wanted to know what was happening to their son but the doctor seemed hesitant. Matthew's parents finally would not take no for an answer and were referred to a doctor specializing in childhood developmental disorders at All-Children's Hospital. They made arrangements to have their son examined.

The specialist's findings, based on her own set of tests, suggested a language delay. Daniel and Ruth wondered if it was autism. The doctor told them it was too early to confirm that type of condition. She recommended speech therapy to help bring his words back and occupational therapy since some of his motor skills were not in the normal range for his age.

Ruth searched for government programs to help pay for the therapies and discovered one called Early Intervention. It would assist with speech and occupational therapy by sending trained therapists to their home. They applied and were accepted.

Speech Therapy is a form of therapy that focuses on speaking ability and understanding speech spoken to the patient. It is used as an aid for children with speech delays as well as adults suffering from brain related ailments such as stroke.[iv]

The other form of therapy Matthew received, occupational therapy, focuses on both physical and mental issues. The therapist challenges the patient at ever increasing levels of task difficulty in order to ultimately have them reach their full potential in a specific skill set.[6]

---

6   Learn more at http://www.centerforautism.com/aba/whatisaba.asp

Signs of Autism

At twenty months, Matthew continued to play quietly by himself. He started lining up his toys into rows and flapping his hands in the air repeatedly. He stared at his parents when they talked to him, a vacant look in his once dancing eyes. His face, before characterized with a wide grin, had now become devoid of any emotion whatsoever. His only form of verbal communication was grunts and groans. He started throwing tantrums with ever increasing intensity and became frustrated very easily.

His retreat into an isolated world of his own was complete. His parents and Pauline couldn't reach him no matter how hard they tried. They didn't want to believe what they were seeing. Daniel and Ruth suddenly felt helpless with what was happening to their son.

One particularly hot summer day, Ruth and Matthew were in the front yard playing with the garden hose. Ruth had dressed him in his bathing suit and he enjoyed getting sprayed by the water. A small flying object caught Ruth's eye and she saw it land on the back of Matthew's neck. As she came closer, she realized it was a bee. It stung her son before she could reach him to swipe it away. She cringed in anticipation of the pain her son would soon endure. His expression didn't change. He simply swatted it off his neck and continued playing in the sprinkler. She ran over to him and looked at the swollen skin around the sting as well as the dying bee. She knew it must have hurt him, but he didn't seem to register any pain whatsoever.

She would see this type of reaction, or lack of reaction to pain, occur again and again. Other examples of this would be when Matthew would jump off the furniture or bounce off a wall and just get back up and continue playing as if nothing had happened. Sometimes he would hurt himself to the point where he couldn't run anymore or even stand back up. Yet, he would continue to try anyway, his face devoid of any hint of pain.

Were the pain messages not reaching her son's brain, or was his brain not interpreting them correctly? She worried that if she didn't constantly watch him carefully, he could inadvertently injure himself at some point.

Out of the Darkness

They talked to the specialist many times, relaying to her what they were witnessing. They would be told again and again that their son was just delayed. Ruth was unable to focus as much as she wanted to on helping her son. She was still very sick much of the time. She continued to recover from her cancer, regularly receiving chemotherapy treatments. When she was feeling up to it, she researched as best she could by herself. All of the behaviors Matthew was exhibiting kept leading her to a single term, autism.

These behaviors included:

- Stemming or self-stimulation - Defined by a wide range of motions involving the hands or arms, it includes everything from slight wrist twitches to full arm motions extending up over the head. The main consistency among all types of stemming is the repetitive behavior associated to them. They can be very minor motions, hardly noticeable or they can be highly pronounced.
- Lining up objects - such as toys, blocks and so on. Consistently lining up objects or stacking them on each other, while sometimes a normal activity, should be carefully observed if done to excess.
- Vacant expressions - even when talked directly to by a parent / caregiver. The child seems distant or disinterested in those around them.
- Side stare - focusing on a single item to the side instead of directly ahead.
- Verbal regression - occurs when the child stops saying the words they have already learned and were using regularly. Their verbal development disintegrates, sometimes to the point of grunts and screams.
- Irregular pain threshold – the child's pain threshold is different from other children and they can inadvertently injure themselves.

Matthew begins to flap his hands repeatedly.

Searching for Answers

After eight month's of speech and occupational therapy with little or no results, Ruth again began to doubt her son was just delayed. It was at this time that she began feeling better from her cancer battle. The months of painful chemotherapy were almost behind her. She would be starting radiation treatments soon and although they were in themselves painful, they were easier for her to handle than the chemo had been. She knew she would have constant pain every day going forward but gathered the strength to begin focusing on saving her son. He was now twenty-three months old and his symptoms continued to worsen.

Ruth read as many books about autism as she could as well as searched the web on the subject. Every time she typed the words 'language delay' into any search engine, page after page of links related to autism kept popping up. This scared her, but she couldn't stop searching.

She and Daniel were continually met with a lot of skepticism from not only Matthew's doctor but from friends as well. Many told them they were blowing things way out of proportion and their son was fine. Daniel and Ruth were told they should trust in the doctors. The doctors had the training and knowledge to understand what was happening and knew what was right for Matthew.

This wore heavily on them both since Daniel and Ruth knew there was nothing wrong with questioning things. They just wanted to know what was truly going on with their son. He had changed so drastically in the last several months and they needed to know why and how to help him. Finally, as a result of Ruth's persistent urging, the specialist at All-Children's relented and ran autism tests on their son. The results of which shattered them emotionally.

A Second Diagnosis

The conclusion was that Matthew was suffering from PDD-NOS or Pervasive Developmental Disorder not otherwise specified – a broad disorder description in the autism spectrum. People that have been observed to display some but not all autistic like characteristics are usually placed within this category.[v] Since these individuals do not fully display all classic autistic symptoms, they can be harder to diagnose until later than those with other autism classifications. What the specialist told them next shocked them both. They were instructed to be ready to institutionalize their son at some point since there was no cure and no rate of recovery.

The doctor told them that although their son was not currently classified as mentally retarded, he would become so in the near future. He would not be able to function in society as an adult and would have to be cared for the rest of his life. They were instructed that they should be realistic and that there was virtually no hope for their son to live a fully enriched and independent life.

Daniel and Ruth were devastated and cried in the office. They had felt that the signs they had seen were warning them of something but to be told point-blank that there was no hope for their son sent them into a state of denial. Questions swirled around in their heads. How had this happened to their wonderful child? Ruth would later recall it as one of the worst days of her life. Daniel's grief over what he had just been told gelled into anger as he realized his son had been given no possible hope whatsoever. He refused to believe there was nothing they could do to help their child.

Daniel stood up and looked at the doctor. "Not my son. Not on my watch." He then walked out of the office followed by Ruth and Matthew. He would find a way. No one was going to tell him it was futile for them to even try.

Intolerance

Matthew's behavior continued to deteriorate. He had a hard time listening to his parents in public and grew increasingly hard to control. Eventually the only way he could voice his objection to something was with grunts and screams. He would tear away from his parents and run.

The stares and scowls of strangers began to wear thin on Daniel and Ruth. People were judging their son as a spoiled little brat. They had no idea what he was going through or why he was behaving the way he was. They showed their disgust in their expressions and body language toward his parents. It made Daniel and Ruth dread going anywhere in public with their child.

One day Ruth, Daniel and Matthew went out to dinner at one of their local favorite Italian restaurants. Ruth had just undergone lasik surgery on her eyes earlier in the day. She decided to have the surgery to help her feel better after her ordeal with cancer. Wearing glasses would be one less thing she would have to concern herself with from now on. She could at least have the comfort of good eyesight.

As soon as they sat down in the restaurant, Matthew started playing. He tapped his metal toy cars, his mother had brought along for him, on the table repeatedly while appearing to stare at the group sitting at the next table. What he was actually doing was watching his cars, from the corner of his eye.

Daniel and Ruth tried to keep him entertained and quiet while they ordered and waited for their food. They were doing a good job but not good enough for those around them. The irritated diners quickly became annoyed with Matthew's behavior even though he wasn't directly bothering anyone. He was just being himself, and a little loud, like any kid his age.

A few harsh, hushed comments were thrown toward Matthew. Daniel and Ruth were told to keep their bratty kid in check. This made Daniel furious. The people judging their son had no idea of Matthew's issues and for them to just openly assume he was a brat made Daniel's blood boil.

Ruth calmed him down before things got too far out of hand but not before Daniel verbally put them in their place. He told them that his son had a developmental disorder and that they should be ashamed of themselves for talking to him and his family in such a manner. It wouldn't be the last time he would have to defend his son's actions in public.

Matthew grew more hyperactive and distant as time went on. He started running up and down aisles in stores not able to pay attention to his mother's attempts to recall him. During these episodes, he would never crash into anyone or knock things down. She noticed him exhibit the same behavior when she took him to the library.

Since he had no physical, outward appearance differences such as those of Downs Syndrome, Fragile X Syndrome or other similar disorders, people just assumed he was spoiled. The piercing, judgmental stares of strangers hurt every time Daniel and Ruth ventured outside their home. Strangers' accusing expressions and often verbal comments swirled around in Ruth's mind.

What a spoiled brat.

What a couple of horrible, ignorant parents.

One day, while Ruth shopped in the clothing section of a local department store, Daniel kept an eye on his son. Matthew repeatedly ran a few steps up the aisle and back to him and Ruth. He needed to process all the things he was seeing and this was how he did it. Ruth continued browsing the clothes in front of her after she and Daniel were sure he wasn't making a scene.

Matthew paused at the aisle next to Daniel's before running back to him. His father immediately noticed the change in his son's demeanor.

"What happened, Matthew?"

His son's eyes skirted to the side toward the aisle he had just come from. Daniel noticed an older woman staring at him and his son with a look of disgust on her face. Matthew stared at the floor, his spirit crushed.

Daniel turned to the woman. "Did you say something to my son?"

"I called him a brat. You should learn to keep him in line. He shouldn't be running up and down, all over the place," was her reply.

At this point Daniel said a few choice words to her out of Matthew's range of hearing. He turned around and walked back to his wife and son.

The woman responded, "I see where he gets it from," along with a few audible curses before walking off. Daniel was furious inside but tempered himself for his son's sake.

Daniel and Ruth decided they would no longer feel that they would have to apologize or leave a situation because of some misguided, judgmental and ignorant person. It wasn't fair to their son or themselves. They had just as much right to be there as anybody else.

Another time, Daniel had to take Ruth in for a follow-up appointment regarding her cancer. Without a sitter available at home for Matthew, they sat in the waiting room. An older man, growing tired of Matthew's running back and forth, made an offer to Daniel.

"I've got a belt here if you need it." He said in all seriousness while gripping the imitation leather around his waist.

Daniel stared at him, the disgust inside reaching the tipping level. "Good, give it here and I'll use it on you." He turned around, biting the rest of his words, and focused his attention on his son in front of him. He didn't want to become angry. The man quickly stopped talking.

Matthew's eyes begin to focus off to the side instead
of directly ahead.

Out of the Darkness

Ruth discovered t-shirts specifically made for autistic children and their parents / caregivers for these types of situations. She located a site and purchased some off the web, making Matthew wear them whenever they went out in public. The shirts simply read 'I'm not a brat. I have autism'.

Another idea she found was to make up business cards that carried basically the same message. She printed some up for her and Daniel to distribute at places such as restaurants and stores when others became annoyed with their son.

Daniel would sometimes 'forget' to give the cards out if people were openly rude to them. He would let Matthew be as loud as he wanted in these cases, not trying to repeatedly quiet him. He was fed up with people judging them and throwing accusing stares everywhere they went.

The shirts and cards didn't last long however. Ruth realized that instead of helping the situation, they were actually making things worse by turning his condition into an excuse. Instead of staring at her son with disgust, people began to stare with pity.

She didn't know which was worse. Neither she nor Daniel certainly wanted anyone's pity or to have their son looked down on as less than a person. While in the beginning the cards and shirts seemed like a way to diffuse situations quickly, Ruth realized that they were actually a message of apology to everyone for the way Matthew was and that others should feel sorry for him.

She concluded that he didn't need an excuse or to apologize for the way he was. He was a wonderful boy, just one with autism. Ruth threw the shirts and cards in the trash as soon as she could, ashamed for buying them in the first place, and vowed never again to make excuses to people about her son's condition.

Autism – A Quick History

Autism diagnosis and treatment is relatively new in the history of known disorders. There are only a few scattered accounts of people behaving in ways now associated as autistic, dating back to the middle-ages. These people were often misunderstood and placed in institutions for the mentally ill, cast out of their communities or suffered worse fates such as death.

Although the term itself has been around since 1911 and was incorrectly believed to be a sub-set of schizophrenia, it wasn't used to classify children with emotional or social difficulties until the early 1940's. That's when American child psychiatrist Leo Kanner noted children he called autistic as all exhibiting a specific set of characteristics in their behavior.

The children appeared:
- hindered in their social interactions
- displayed anxiety over change
- seemed to exhibit good memory skills
- came from talented families
- repeated sounds and phrases they had heard many hours after the fact
- were over-sensitive to certain stimuli such as noise
- suffered digestive problems

Then in 1944, German Hans Asperger, wrote about children he examined in studies independent of Kanner. Many of the characteristics he noticed in the children were similar, if not the same to Kanner's findings. He also noticed that the children he studied seemed to have speech skills but impaired motor function.

Autism understanding took a turn for the worse when a University of Chicago professor, Bruno Bettelheim, latched onto a phrase first proposed by Leo Kanner. His views on the subject took many by surprise. Kanner had theorized the reason for autistic behavior in children had to do with their mothers. His belief was that autistic children had not received enough nurturing and affection and therefore had retreated into their own worlds. They were unable to build social skills due to their mothers not reinforcing bonds with them early in life.

His method of therapy to help these children was to separate them from their mothers and/or family's entirely. Mothers of autistic children were suddenly blamed in society as being bad and many began to think of them as causing the problems their children were experiencing. They were called 'refrigerator moms' since they were apparently cold to their child's needs. Though Kanner is credited with coining the phrase, Bettelheim brought it to mainstream thinking.[vi]

We now know this couldn't be further from the truth. This way of thinking took the forefront in much autism research through the 1960's and 1970's. Many in the scientific community would eventually come to challenge it.

It wasn't until the 1980's and 1990's that behavior therapy became the primary focus in treatment options for autism. Links to a person's genetic code were discovered but environmental factors also appeared to be an issue as well.

As more understanding developed, it became known that autism is more a spectrum disorder and not a specific set of symptoms. Children or adults can fall anywhere along the spectrum to varying degrees from very mild to extremely severe. This is one of the reasons why it has been hard to define over the decades.

Today, it is one of the fastest growing developmental disabilities in the world. It affects one in every one hundred and fifty children. Afflicting boys more often than girls by a shocking four to one ratio, it strikes one in every ninety-eight boys. The effects are usually life-long.[vii]

Radiation Therapy

A month after Ruth's last chemotherapy treatment, the final remnants of the chemicals dissipated from her system. Although Ruth would continue to have chronic pain in her chest, her anxiety and panic attacks began to fade. Her hair began growing back in and she slowly regained her appetite. The doctors' attempted reconstructive surgery again, and again her body rejected it.

Her port and expanders became painfully infected and it was decided that removing them would be the best option at the time. Normally, port-acaths are kept in a patient for five to ten years in the event of a relapse. Because of her infections, forcing her into the hospital often, it was deemed safer to remove the port and expanders instead and begin the radiation therapy portion of her treatment.

While her doctors wanted Ruth to feel good about herself emotionally, as that would play a major role in her recovery, they felt they would have to wait and readdress the matter of reconstructive surgery after they had taken care of her cancer fully.

Permanent tattoo markers where inked into the skin of her chest so that the radiation technicians could line up their equipment. Less intrusive than chemotherapy, each session lasted fifteen minutes a day, five days a week for seven weeks.

The tissues in her chest were burned by the radiation, causing them to tighten and become permanently hardened. Each treatment painfully squeezed her chest tissues tighter together and that tightness and sharp stabbing pain would never go away.

It constantly made itself known especially if she outstretched an arm to reach for something. Even tasks she thought nothing of in the past such as typing on a computer keyboard became long and painful. Still, with all the pain, she was thankful to be over her chemotherapy.

Room for Hope

At thirty months, Matthew was still not showing any progress with speech and occupational therapies. His parents had been hopeful since there had been improvement in some children after undergoing these forms of treatment.

In Matthew's case however, his development actually continued to regress. Distressed and no longer having to spend time recovering from chemotherapy treatments, Ruth began heavily researching on her own and one day in the library discovered a book titled <u>Let Me Hear Your Voice</u> by Catherine Maurice. It focused on a promising supplemental therapy called Applied Behavioral Analysis or ABA for short.

Designed as a goal-oriented type of therapy, it allowed for true milestones to be seen quickly. The child is given some type of challenge such as a puzzle. They are then provided either the solution or clues to it for which they receive a reward upon proper completion. If they do not succeed or go off task, they are redirected to the challenge again. Positive reinforcement is a key factor in ABA therapy. Once children master skills, they can then begin to apply them to their natural surroundings and 'learn how to learn'.

Doctors working with UCLA had conducted sessions with autistic children with proven and documented success. Each child in the case study had received forty hours of ABA therapy per week across a number of weeks and the results were impressive.[viii]

This made sense to Ruth and she was very excited. She immediately began using the techniques she had read about in the book to help her son tackle toilet training. After a day of positive reinforcement, placing 'targets' in the bowl and running the sink water, her son had gotten the gist of what he needed to do. She was thrilled that she had been able to get through to him and knew ABA therapy would help him in ways nothing they had tried before could.

Daniel and Ruth immediately contacted Florida's Early Intervention program to have this type of therapy incorporated into their son's treatments. This was roughly twelve months after he had begun speech and occupational therapy. They were eager to see what progress he could make.

It took them by surprise when they were told that they could not try this method with their son. It was 'unconventional' and 'unproven'. Undaunted, Ruth called daily to request this type of therapy be approved for her son.

After about a month and a half, Early Intervention finally relented. The woman she had talked with on the phone said that even though she didn't believe it would work, she would approve it because Matthew's window of aid with them would be up soon. She was also tired of Ruth calling her.

Even at only two hours a week, Daniel and Ruth began to notice their son quickly making progress. He started to venture further out of the isolated world he had shrunk into and began saying words.

The days rolled around to his third birthday. He was speaking at a fourteen month old level but his parents were thrilled to see him speaking at all. It had been over a year since they had heard anything from him other than grunts and screams. An elated Ruth asked the ABA therapist to encourage Matthew to speak more and she incorporated a greater emphasis on speech oriented goal skills into her ABA program for him.

Matthew suddenly seemed to be moving in the right direction again. Ruth called the specialist to have her son re-evaluated. Because he had improved greatly, the doctor removed his autism status and reclassified him as developmentally delayed. This was a diagnosis Ruth didn't agree with but could do nothing about.

Teaching the Teachers

The time eventually came when Early Intervention would discontinue at home therapy sessions. Matthew was three years old now and in order to continue receiving benefits going forward, Ruth and Daniel would have to place him in the public school system.

The Florida Diagnostic and Learning Resources System (FDLRS) also known as 'Fiddlers', would automatically provide assistance once in the school system. This statewide organization provides diagnostic and instructional support services to teachers, parents, therapists, school administrators and students.[ix] As of 2008, FDLRS contained nineteen associate centers each serving up to nine school districts.

Daniel and Ruth struggled to locate a school that had the necessary training and faculty to help their son continue to progress. Once they found an adequate school, they requested ABA therapy sessions be administered during Matthew's school day. Ruth had mentioned how her son had started speaking again and come out of his isolation with ABA.

To their dismay, the school's special needs administrator scoffed at them stating that they should know Florida doesn't pay for ABA. She told them their son would only be eligible to receive speech and occupational therapy at school. Daniel and Ruth were powerless to stop her in the decision. They decided to continue Matthew's weekly ABA sessions at home on their own. During each session, Ruth watched the therapist intently. She would go over the exercises with Matthew again on his off days to reinforce what he had learned.

Ruth felt her son was not enjoying the school. Matthew, unable to speak to his parents, communicated his dread at going in other ways. After just his third day at the new school, he began throwing up every morning. At first Ruth thought he was just trying to adjust but as the behavior continued, she became more and more alarmed.

She asked his teacher if everything was okay and was told yes. They didn't feel this to be true and that, coupled with the cold manner in which the faculty treated them, made them think otherwise. They listened to what their son was showing them instead and came to the conclusion that

Matthew would be better off somewhere else. Daniel and Ruth finally decided to remove their son.

Daniel racked his brain for an alternative, researching several schools before finally remembering how one of Matthew's prior therapists had been a pre-kindergarten teacher. He called her up one afternoon and asked her about the school she taught at. After the call he made arrangements to tour the school.

This faculty seemed to have a better attitude and Daniel and Ruth signed Matthew up to attend. As fate would have it, his former therapist became his teacher. His vomiting abruptly stopped and he became eager to go every day. He attended class there for a year doing daily activities such as circle time, playing with toys, building crafts as well as speech and occupational therapy.

As the school year came to an end, Ruth arranged a meeting with their son's teacher and a counselor to discuss the next year's curricula and progress plan for her son. She was told that Matthew would be enrolled in the same class he had been in the prior school year, under the same teacher. He would be doing the same activities over again and would not be given the opportunity to advance until first or second grade even if he seemed ready to do so.

This upset Ruth. In her mind, the school was basically behaving like a baby-sitter instead of a learning institution. They tried to reassure Ruth by telling her that her son would be re-evaluated when he turned five years old, two years away! Ruth disagreed, deciding that she would have to do something. As much as she and Daniel disliked it, they knew it was time to look for another school again.

They started calling other schools and talking with people who might know of a good place that would work with their son. A good resource turned out to be their son's ABA therapist. She mentioned a school in the Orlando area, over an hour and a half away that utilized ABA therapy in the classroom itself. This was something they had advocated but could not get support for from the beginning. It was a new charter school specializing in helping autistic children and only accepted a total of two hundred and fifty students annually in order to keep class sizes low and be able to assist each of its students fully.

They immediately called and were put on a waiting list for possible enrollment. After several weeks of waiting they received a phone call informing them that their son would be accepted for the 2004-05 school year.

Happy and without a second thought, they immediately put their house up for sale and made preparations to move to the Orlando area.

They found a residence in a nice neighborhood that they believed was close to Matthew's new school. What they didn't realize was that with Orlando's thick, traffic choked roads they would still be over an hour away from it in driving time.

After several months of shuttling her son to and from his school, Ruth's fatigue caught up to her. Even though she had been in remission for her cancer, the fight she had put up had lingering affects causing her pain daily. In many ways, she was still recovering from her own ordeal herself.

Although she didn't like the prospect, she and Daniel looked into bussing their son even though they worried he might be teased or misunderstood. Bussing also meant that his morning commute would increase to an hour and a half and his afternoon ride home to over two hours since the bus had to stop in various neighborhoods along the way. It wasn't a straight shot there and back as it was when his mother drove him. Ruth didn't like agreeing to it but in the end had to for her own health.

One of the first things his new teacher had scheduled on her class's itinerary was teaching the children how to write the alphabet. She showed them how to draw the letter A and planned two full weeks for each letter to give the students a solid foundation at their age. Matthew noticed the front of the classroom had mini posters above the chalkboard. They displayed each letter of the alphabet in order. He began to draw them himself and finished learning the letter Z while the rest of the class was focusing on D. Every letter after A, he had taught himself by looking at the posters and drawing what he saw.

Warning

One day, Ruth noticed Matthew drawing intently on a piece of paper with a crayon. He was almost four years old. The picture took him less than a minute to draw and when he was done, she could clearly see what it was. He had drawn a tele-tubby from memory in exacting detail. The drawing looked as if a child twice his age had drawn it. She was in awe and showed Daniel who was also amazed. They decided to give him a sketch pad. He filled it within the week and they began buying more.

Soon his love of animals really became evident. He would quickly draw them, after visiting the zoo or watching them on television, in great detail for his age. The sketch books his mother had purchased for him quickly filled with all sorts of wonderful creatures.

He sketched everything from rhinos to howler monkeys. He seemed to draw them with ease in minutes and one could easily tell what they were just by looking at them. This amazed his parents and teachers as well since he had never had a class on drawing. He just inherently drew extremely well.

In addition to drawing pictures, Matthew started writing words. One day he wrote the word 'WARNING' down. The letters were very well formed and, similar to his drawings, appeared as if a much older child had written them. Ruth would see him write the word several times over the next few weeks. Each time he wrote it down, he would point at it and ask 'what' as if to ask "what is this?"

Ruth didn't understand but pronounced the word for him each time he wrote it. She had no idea where he picked up the word from although she had seen him, on several occasions, staring at magazine covers laying about the house. He didn't really pay attention to pictures, since none of them contained animals, only the letters making up the words. She thought this a little strange since he hadn't learned to read yet. It alarmed her a little that he would fixate on that word in particular.

While driving on an errand one day, with Matthew in the back-seat, Ruth pulled down her visor to block the sun's glare from her eyes. Matthew immediately spelled the word and she looked up. In front of her, clear as day, was the word 'WARNING' in big red letters on the back of the visor. Her visor contained the generic alert, to keep kids in the backseat at all times while driving. She looked at her son in the mirror in amazement. He had seen the word and wrote it down so many times perfectly from memory hours after riding in the car.

He started noticing other words and would repeat his new skill countless times over. Each new word amazed his parents. They were not small words but big, complicated ones with many letters that he seemed to recall with ease hours later and write down extremely well. Papers around the house began filling with words such as AMBULANCE, WALGREENS and UNIVERSAL. He enjoyed writing the words over and over again.

Autism Cannot Be Overcome

Daniel and Ruth had been very active parents, wanting to be involved as much as possible in their son's continuing development. They regularly attended monthly parent / teacher group meetings. During each meeting the director would present news and project updates on what the school was doing to help the autistic children in its care. This same person would also always stress that parents not try what she called 'un-tested' or 'pseudo' therapies.

In her opinion, no diet or nutritional therapies should ever be attempted, period. She continually preached that autism was non-recoverable. Other parents were informed that their children would likely need life improvement classes in their high-school years so they could, if fortunate, get a factory job somewhere or some other similar position. Their children would not be able to attend mainstream high school classes or have the slightest chance of going to college.

It all reminded Daniel of the specialist that finally diagnosed their son with autism. Here was a school mandated to help these children and its faculty kept drilling the parents over and over again to not hope for a better life. Ruth and Daniel didn't agree with the philosophy but kept Matthew in the school because he was progressing.

Someone on Their Side

In the summer of 2005, during one of his countless on-line research sessions, Daniel stumbled across information regarding a doctor by the name of Mary Megson. She caught his interest because she only specialized in children with autism. What surprised him was that she felt its affects could be lessened and in some cases removed altogether through vitamin and nutritional therapy.[7x]

She was a member of an organization he had never heard of called Defeat Autism Now (DAN). A collection of professionals dedicated to the exploration, evaluation and dissemination of scientifically documented biomedical interventions related to autism utilizing the efforts of clinicians, researchers and parents. [8]

What got Daniel and Ruth so excited was the fact that she had spoken before Congress with verifiable data of treatments and therapies used to help recover children.

Neither Daniel nor Ruth had ever heard anyone even mention the word recovery when speaking of autism. It was something they always believed in but could never gain support for, not from the doctors, their friends or in some cases even their own extended family. Here was a reputable doctor not only discussing its validity before Congress but showing it as highly possible as long as the doctors were allowed to do clinical trails to support their individual findings.

Daniel quickly typed up an email informing Dr. Megson of his son, who was now four and a half years old, and asked if she could help him. When she replied with interest, Daniel knew he had to have her meet his son. Within a month Ruth and Matthew were on a plane flying over seven hundred and fifty miles away to meet Dr. Megson at her clinic in Richmond, Virginia. Although he wished to join his wife and son, Daniel could only afford to send Ruth and Matthew.

Prior to their meeting, Dr. Megson sent a test kit for Ruth to complete and mail back. This would allow them to discuss the doctor's findings fully

---

7   A transcript of Dr. Megson's report before Congress appears at the end of this book.
8   Learn more about Defeat Autism Now at http://www.defeatautismnow.com

and make the most of their one and only physical meeting. Samples of urine, bowel movements and hair were taken. Matthew's blood was withdrawn at a local lab facility also.

Dr. Megson had the results when Ruth and Matthew walked into her office. Ruth was horrified to discover highly toxic levels of mercury, lead and arsenic in her son's blood. His testosterone levels were extremely elevated as well.

Matthew played in the corner with his favorite toy while his mother discussed the findings with the doctor. The conversation turned toward nutrition and Dr. Megson inquired if Ruth had attempted vitamin supplements with Matthew. She didn't know that could help him and so hadn't pursued it.

After observing him playing for a few moments, Dr. Megson noticed Matthew staring at things in the room from the corner of his eye. He would look at the wall while playing with his favorite toy. She suggested immediately starting him on cod liver oil, a natural and rich source of vitamin A, vital for healthy eyesight.[xi]

She also recommended B-12 and some other supplements as well. It was suggested that Ruth begin with one supplement and, barring any ill effects, continue adding new ones at a frequency of one every other week. She would also need to carefully record the effects each supplement had on her son, both positive and negative, in order to assess which ones were helping him and which ones had little or no affect.

Ruth asked why vitamin supplements might help and Dr. Megson explained that natural vitamin A was lacking in Mathew's diet. Vitamin A, normally liquid at room temperature, had been in recent decades turned into a solid due to cheap and inefficient food processing procedures. Receptors allowing cells to communicate to each other break down without natural vitamin A. Dr. Megson had seen recovery in patients once they had begun vitamin A supplements.

One of the many aspects of autism is the inability of the body to absorb or fully process certain vitamins and minerals. Because of this, the brain doesn't get the proper nutrients it needs to remain healthy and therefore malfunctions. These malfunctions are then displayed as autism. Adding vitamin supplements in moderation to Matthew's daily nutritional intake shouldn't hurt him so long as they were properly monitored; they should only help him.

Ruth was instructed to make sure whatever they gave him contained no additional preservatives as these could hinder his progress. The cod liver oil needed to be certified as mercury free. He would also need to receive regular check ups to make sure his vitamin intake didn't exceed healthy standards for his age and weight. B-12 would need to be given in injection form since that was the most efficient way to introduce it into the body.

Dr. Megson also inquired as to whether or not they had tried chelation with Matthew. Ruth had never heard of the term. Chelation is the introduction of binding agents into the body in order to allow toxic metals, such as mercury, to combine with them. The resulting substance can then be purged from the patient's system. Heavy metals in the body that can not be removed by other methods bind or stick to these agents and are then flushed out either naturally by the patient or intravenously by a licensed physician.

Developed during World War II as a way to assist Navy divers in detoxifying their bodies after years of painting ship hulls, the procedures and agents used have grown more efficient over the years. It is no longer just used to remove large doses of metals from the body.

Children with autism show minute doses of heavy metals in their systems that need removal. Due to their genetic make-up, they are more susceptible than others to the affects of having these toxins in their body.

Chelation is now classified in two separate forms. They are hard chelation, the direct introduction of chemicals into the blood for the purpose of binding with and expelling heavy metals from the body, and soft chelation, a more subtle introduction of chemical compounds that can be administered topically.

Of the two, Dr. Megson urged Ruth to ease her son onto soft or natural chelation. This consisted of creams and sprays that could be purchased at local health food stores. When absorbed by the skin, they would bind to any toxic metals in his system.

Dr. Megson had opted against recommending hard chelation for Matthew after noticing the silver amalgam fillings in his mouth. She was afraid that the process, in the natural course of doing its job, could potentially leech the toxic mercury out of his fillings and into his body instead.

As can be expected, soft chelation agents do not work quite as fast as FDA approved hard chelation techniques. These include suppositories or intravenous chelation. With soft chelation, however, there was no possible risk of leeching occurring from Matthew's silver fillings. His parents started him on soft chelation as soon as he and Ruth returned home.

Daniel and Ruth would later read that amalgam fillings constantly emit mercury vapors in the mouth especially when a person consumes hot foods or liquids.[xii] These vapors could then theoretically be absorbed into the bloodstream and distributed throughout the rest of the body.

Dr. Megson strongly urged Ruth to have the mercury replaced with composite resin fillings as soon as possible. The request proved much harder to fulfill than Daniel and Ruth thought it would be. They had a difficult time locating a doctor willing to remove the original fillings and replace them. It would take a full year before they could locate someone agreeing to do so, because the procedure had potential risks. Dental dams had to be inserted into Matthew's mouth so that any loose fillings or pieces of them didn't wind up being ingested by accident once removed from his teeth. Such an incident could harm his already toxic body.

Once the amalgam is removed, it has to be placed in a special hazardous chemical waste container and disposed of properly. Any water source containing mercury measurements greater than 2 parts per billion is deemed hazardous to animal and plant life. It is readily absorbed by fish and other wildlife and can be passed both directly and indirectly to humans.[xiii] If the amount of silver from a single filling falls into a small lake, by law a hazmat team is supposed to be called in to clean it up and the lake is quarantined from all pedestrian traffic. This amount times four was in their son's mouth!

One final thing Dr. Megson suggested was to alter Matthew's nutritional intake. She asked Ruth if she had heard of the gluten-casein diet and if not, she and her husband should look into it. The gluten-casein diet removes all wheat gluten and dairy from a person's nutritional intake as a way to keep these hard to process proteins from disrupting his or her system.

The diet had been brought to Dr. Megson's attention by the mother of an autistic child that had noticed good results with it. Many autistic patients' bodies can not break down gluten or casein fully before it enters the bloodstream. This results in opiates being released into the blood. In some cases children hallucinate as if on some sort of high. They become addicted and have to be gradually weaned off these proteins. Taking them off successfully can result in better sleep and less hyperactivity among other things.[xiv]

Dr. Megson had recorded successful results in other autistic children exposed to this type of diet. She told Ruth to be diligent since she was too far away to help. The doctor encouraged her to regularly keep in touch both by phone and through email. The meeting lasted over three hours. Ruth was very thankful for Dr. Megson's insight and eager to get home and see if what she had learned would help her son.

Setting Things in Motion

Once home, Ruth slowly began introducing two to three vitamins every few weeks to Matthew, administered three times a day. She observed their affects before continuing and eventually worked her way up to eight different supplements. It only took a couple of weeks for Ruth to see a difference in her son. Issues for Matthew, such as constipation and gas, normalized. He was able to focus better and his hyperactivity lessened.

She gradually progressed in Matthew's treatment, making sure the vitamins she introduced had no residual negative effects. Supplements that didn't help him within a week or two were removed in favor of adding new ones that might.

Vitamin A appeared to help with his sight. Ruth noticed that he no longer viewed things from the corner of his eye. Cod liver oil seemed to help him pay attention for longer lengths of time. When his parents spoke to him he began facing them and staring as though he were trying to focus on their words and faces. He would sit longer periods to watch television or draw. Gone were the days of jumping up every few seconds to run around the room.

Supplemental Melatonin, a hormone naturally produced by the body to aid in sleep, didn't seem to help Matthew. Ruth found studies in her research in which people had similar issues with sleep. Melatonin had worked for them but only after the liver had been cleansed. Upon discovering that dandelion root and milk thistle aid in healthy liver function, she added these supplements to his diet. As soon as Ruth felt Matthew's liver was detoxified, she tried Melatonin again. He slept soundly through the night.

Before this breakthrough, he would restlessly sleep an hour then wake for two or three more before falling back down in complete exhaustion. With Daniel working overnights, this was extremely taxing on Ruth. Every night was spent trying to get him calmed down enough to go back to bed.

Matthew's stemming lessened. Vitamin B-6 decreased his hyperactivity. He stopped jumping off the couch and crashing into furniture, a common daily activity before vitamin therapy. He also stopped running away as frequently during outings to the store. His practice of sprinting up and down the aisles, although still there, lessened in frequency. His parents were excited to see the changes taking place in their son's behavior.

Ruth continued introducing new supplements at regular intervals. Tocopherol monoglucoside (TMG) – a water soluble Vitamin E derivative, helped him increase his working vocabulary somewhat. He still continued to say one or two words at a time with prompting but he was at least saying more of them.

Daniel and Ruth tried hard for several weeks to get him on the gluten-casein diet. It was challenging to locate alternatives to the myriad products on the market that contained either one or the other of the proteins they were attempting to avoid. Matthew always had been a very picky eater and in many instances threw fits and began starving rather than eating what they prepared for him.

Eventually, he did start eating some of the items on the diet after much coaxing. Ruth finally decided that she would either continue with the diet or the supplements but couldn't go on with both. Together they were too expensive. Since he was still fighting the diet, she dropped it in favor of continuing on with the supplements.

Issues with School

Matthew began his second year in pre-kindergarten with a new teacher. His previous teacher, who he had built a comfortable relationship with, left the school to further her career elsewhere. Her replacement was very inexperienced in teaching autistic kids. Daniel and Ruth would find out later that it was her first year with special needs children and that she was learning as she went.

As his vitamin therapy continued, Mathew's new teacher sent home more and more favorable reports. She had noticed gradual changes in Matthew's behavior, most notably his ability to sit still and focus more in class. Daniel and Ruth were pleased with his progress and a few weeks later mentioned to her that they had started Matthew on vitamin therapy. The very next day he brought home a bad report. It would be the first of many. Each one seemed worse than the last. They were shocked to read that their son would cry and carry on for hours at a time, having breakdown after breakdown.

Daniel and Ruth thought this somewhat strange since his behavior at home still consistently showed the same improvement. He had never had a tantrum last longer than a few minutes. They couldn't believe what they were reading from his teacher. After a couple of weeks of the reports, they urgently inquired for a meeting with the school administrator. When they realized that the meeting was going to resolve nothing, they asked to review the classroom video tapes of their son during the times in question.

One of the nice things about the school was that all classroom sessions were recorded and archived. After sitting through several minutes of video they discovered Matthew's trigger for becoming upset. His behavior changed when his teacher placed headphones on his ears for occupational therapy. He cried a total of five minutes fighting to get them off. What the teacher failed to realize was that Matthew has an aversion to anything covering his ears, part of the sensitivity to touch issue that some autistic children experience. Doing such a thing to him is like raking fingernails across a chalkboard for most other people. She didn't understand this and thought he was just being difficult with her.

Out of the Darkness

Daniel and Ruth were very upset with the way the teacher handled the situation and questioned the incident. Afterward, the teacher was trained on how to notice these signs in autistic children and how to calm them. The training didn't help. Daniel and Ruth continued to receive poor daily progress reports and they noticed their son begin dreading school again.

Although they didn't like it, Daniel and Ruth kept Matthew in the school for the time being since he was making progress. He had begun counting and adding more words to his vocabulary. Daniel decided to keep any talk of therapy out of his conversations with the teachers and faculty from then on. After a month, the reports started turning favorable again.

Matthew's parents kept searching for an alternative and finally located a small school near home for him to attend instead. That one didn't work either so Ruth withdrew him a week later.

Although uncomfortable about it, she decided to home school her son until she and Daniel could find a more adequate environment. Matthew was tutored at home from January to summer break of 2006. Educating him at home was difficult for Ruth. Matthew had a hard time focusing and staying on lesson tasks. He associated mom with playtime not work. He didn't understand why she had suddenly changed.

As the summer progressed, so did the stress Daniel and Ruth were feeling. August was closing in fast and they had not been able to find a suitable replacement school. Matthew would need to go into kindergarten soon. Daniel inquired everywhere trying to locate a school with low class sizes, teacher aides and a curriculum that catered to special needs children.

A friend at the hotel Daniel worked at told him of an exciting new school in the area. It sounded exactly like what he and Ruth had been looking for. As soon as he could, he called up its admissions office to begin the enrollment process for his son.

Matthew was enrolled just in time for the beginning of the fall 2006 session. All daily reports were good and he was enjoying school again.

Seizures

In October of 2006, Matthew's parents decided to take him to Disneyworld. The day was fun for Matthew. He took in everything, dragging his parents from attraction to attraction. During the Snow White ride he suddenly became very scared, clinging to his mother for reassurance through to the end. After the ride was over, he seemed fine again. They enjoyed the rest of the day forgetting about the incident.

That night Daniel and Ruth awoke to deafening screams coming from Matthew's room. When they ran in, they saw their son soaking wet with sweat. Ruth was sure he had just had a bad dream. As the weeks progressed however, the screams continued and were eventually joined by uncontrollable, violent convulsions.

Matthew's eyes would become wide and unresponsive and nothing they did or said could help him. Daniel and Ruth were frightened for their son, never having seen him this way before. He was worsening to the point where it appeared to them that he was having seizures. Each time they ran into his room, it took several minutes before they could bring him out of an episode to focus on them again.

Daniel began researching to locate the best neurological doctors available to them through their insurance. He was able to arrange a meeting with a leading neurologist in Naples, Florida.

They told the doctor of Matthew's autistic classification and everything that had happened to him. After listening intently, the neurologist told them, in all honesty, that he didn't know how he could help. Autism was not his specialty. He said that the episode they described sounded like seizures to him but he just couldn't be sure without viewing one for himself. Before they left his office, he mentioned he would put them in contact with neurologist better equipped to assist with autism.

Daniel received an email the very next day with three hospital recommendations. One was with Shand's Hospital at the University of Florida in Gainesville. Daniel had attempted to have Matthew seen by the doctors at Shand's before going to Naples. It had been recently labeled as one of the top fifty hospitals in over eleven specialties in the entire United States.[xv]

However, he was told they could only see his son by referral. He now had one and called them up. An appointment was scheduled.

The doctors decided to keep Matthew in the hospital for a total of three days. During that time they performed a battery of tests on him. Daniel had to continue working during this time but Ruth stayed with their son, day and night. In order to pass the hours between tests, Ruth brought some movies she knew her son enjoyed, to view with him in his room.

The night after watching one of them, he woke up screaming with many identical symptoms Ruth had witnessed at home. The doctors ran more tests noticing no abnormalities. They finally determined that he was suffering from severe night terrors induced from what he had seen during his waking hours.

The hospital, feeling they had found the root of the problem, removed Matthew's autism classification. They replaced it with a severe receptive language disorder instead. Their main reasoning for removing the autism classification was his unusual display of affection. He consistently hugged and gave his mother kisses in front of the medical staff. The doctors echoed what Matthew's first pediatrician had said. Autistic children are usually not very affectionate even to family members.

After three days of tests, Matthew was prescribed forty hours a week of speech therapy and discharged. Happy his son was not having seizures Daniel questioned the speech delayed label. Matthew still showed classic signs of autism such as stemming and lining up toys. The conclusion was that while it was true that Matthew displayed autistic-like qualities, he was in fact not autistic. An analysis from a leading hospital meant a lot and gave Ruth and Daniel hope. According to the hospital, with the proper speech therapy, their son could possibly recover to live a full and rewarding life.

Ruth set a meeting with Matthew's school administrator. She brought up what had happened and what Shands had recommended, requesting her son receive forty hours of speech therapy weekly. The administrator told her that the school was not obligated to follow the recommendation, but would consider it and get back to her. Nothing came of the request and to Ruth and Daniel's dismay, their son's speech therapy sessions remained at two and a half hours per week.

A New Hope

In November of 2006 while cleaning up the kitchen counter, Daniel discovered a letter from Dr. Megson in Virginia. In the letter she inquired how Matthew was progressing. Ruth had not mentioned the letter to Daniel. It suggested a new and hopeful therapy. This new treatment was very expensive and Ruth was sure it was well out of their financial range. In the letter, the doctor mentioned Hyperbaric Oxygen treatments, or HBOT, for autism. Daniel had never heard of the therapy but wanted to learn as much as possible. He began researching and grew excited as he uncovered more.

Hyperbaric therapy had actually been around since 1662. In that year, an English physician named Henshaw constructed a device which he labeled the domicilium. It consisted of a rudimentary metal chamber that used organ bellows to either increase or decrease the interior pressure of the device.

He documented, what he considered, many successful breakthroughs with his new invention even though it had very little pressure to push oxygen into the body.[xvi] Others began to try their hand at the technology and favorable reports of hyperbaric therapy continued throughout the years. Modifications and improvements upon Henshaw's original concept as well as newer materials and technology helped progress HBOT therapy.

In the 1950's, a Dutch physician by the name of Boerema, published his extensive research regarding hyperbaric use in surgery. He documented case studies in which the therapy had aided in the recovery of several conditions. He is known in some circles as the father of modern hyperbaric medicine.[xvii]

A closely working associate of his discovered that anaerobic bacteria that thrived in low oxygen environments in the body could be controlled by HBOT technology.

The United States Military – the Navy in particular – began researching it heavily around this same time frame. They were looking for ways to allow divers the ability to remain at depth for longer periods of time without side-effects.

Out of the Darkness

Mild chamber units were introduced in the early 1990's with the introduction of the Gamow bag. Invented by an avid outdoorsman, the predecessor to the mild chamber unit was only big enough to fit a single person and utilized a foot pump to inflate. Its main goal was to be carried by hikers for treating altitude sickness on location.[xviii] Coming down from high elevations too quickly could make climbers very sick or potentially kill them. Carrying a chamber to places of extreme altitude had proven to save lives over the years. Its design and ingenuity opened the door to more affordable and accessible hyperbaric treatment for the masses. As the materials and technology improved, the benefits of HBOT became more widespread.

He read about a young mother who, along with her baby, had suffered dangerous levels of carbon monoxide poisoning in their home. HBOT had not only prevented their deaths, but had brought them both back to full health in a matter of hours. People who had been severely burned had had their injuries fully healed in weeks with no scaring whatsoever. Sufferers of Parkinson's disease were able to enjoy life for the first time in years.[xix]

It became a method of treatment for the wealthy and for athletes engaged in professional sports, many of which use it extensively today to significantly increase injury recovery rates.

Hyperbarics and Autism Treatment

Daniel and Ruth conducted a search, finally locating the nearest DAN doctor in Florida working with hyperbarics. His name was Dr. Dan Rossignol and he had a family medical practice ninety miles away on the east coast, in Melbourne Florida.

A recent Florida transplant, having completed his medical schooling at the Medical College of Virginia; he specialized in the treatment of autism through hyperbaric chambers. He had conducted human trials on the subject with great results, successfully treating patients since 2004.

Daniel called the doctor's office and arranged two weeks of chamber therapy to begin in mid December. Ruth wondered how they could afford that many treatments. She decided to give it a try for her husband's sake. She didn't believe two weeks would do much for their son since the doctor had mentioned most patients hadn't seen results until after approximately forty treatments. Daniel had asked her to just try. It couldn't hurt, only help. If there was even the slightest hope that it could work, they owed it to their son. She went along not wanting to dash his hopes.

They discovered that Dr. Rossignol had stumbled onto hyperbaric therapy as a means to help his own kids. Both his children had been diagnosed with autism. At first, he had listened to others in the medical community who he felt were more informed on the subject than he was. When he mentioned his wife had heard about hyperbarics many felt it unreliable, some even calling it a useless avenue for him to consider pursuing.

His wife uncovered an obscure control study of hyperbaric use in autism patients. That and a few other, hard to find, scattered papers helped him make up his mind. He and his wife decided to try it, since there was virtually no risk that their children could be harmed by following the treatment.

After his fortieth treatment, their older son, who had been only saying single words, approached him and said "open the gate, please." He was referring to the small children's gate protecting the kids from falling down the stairs in their house. Rossignol was so astonished he nearly fell over. The only thing that they had altered in his son's treatments was the inclusion of hyperbaric oxygen therapy. In that moment, he was convinced something great was happening. His son soon began stringing words into full sentences with alarming clarity. His younger son quickly followed suit as well.

Rossignol was excited to see his children open up to the world around them. It was as if they were coming back to life in front of his eyes. Although he knew something had happened, he couldn't figure out what exactly it was that had helped them. Had it been the increase in oxygen or in pressure? Could it have been a combination of both?

Pressure appeared to help with inflammation. There had been numerous cases in which inflammation had been greatly diminished as a result of hyperbaric use. Autism appears to be linked to inflammation in the brain so it would make sense that an anti-inflammatory measure like HBOT could help.

Oxygen, increases inflammation except when accompanied by pressure. It also opens up blood vessels and kills bacteria that thrive in O2-poor systems. Environments, such as the anaerobic type found in the digestive tracts of many autistic persons, can benefit with an increase in oxygen. Another possible reason for his sons' progress is that HBOT stimulates the production of adult stem cells, the body's natural healers.

Based on the research he had done as well as the remarkable turn-around he had witnessed with his own children, Rossignol started incorporating HBOT at his clinic. He wanted to help other children afflicted with autism or other neurological ailments such as stroke, cerebral palsy and near drowning.

Daniel inquired as to why chelation or hyperbaric therapy hadn't even been suggested to him before. Rossignol offered a possible explanation. He had noticed that many doctors and health professionals lacked knowledge regarding legitimate alternate autism resources and therapies.

While in medical school, he had been taught chelation killed people and hyperbaric therapy was this era's snake oil remedy, referring to the useless vials of colored water peddled as cure-alls by traveling salesmen in olden times. It did nothing to help people and should not be recommended to any future patients.

He discovered these claims to be largely untrue as he began to witness time and again breakthroughs his colleagues and himself made with them.

He conducted structured, safe clinical trials with hyperbarics on over one hundred patients and saw first-hand how they benefited from the treatments they had received.

An increase in oxygen saturation in the blood eases oxidative stress and inflammation, two characteristics of autistic individuals.[xx] He began posting peer review papers trying to get the word out and has been doing so ever since.[9]

---

9 Details related to the benefits of HBOT for autism can be found at http://www.biomedcentral.com/1471-2431/7/36

Like Flying in a Plane

Matthew's therapy would consist of him being closely monitored while resting in a pressurized oxygen hyperbaric chamber for two hours a day, five days a week. Hard chambers were a more expensive therapy and pressurized between six to eight pounds per square inch, allowing the occupant to breath one hundred percent oxygen. They must be used only under strict supervised control by trained professionals in a registered facility due to issues that could arise without careful guidance.

Mild hyperbaric chambers, a less costly alternative, pressurize at one point three atmospheres supplying about thirty to thirty-five percent oxygen to the body. There is virtually no chance of injury to the occupant and because the oxygen content is not at one hundred percent, minimal chance of fire.

The unit consists of an eight by three and a half foot inflatable chamber that rests over a rigid, metal skeleton. The inside air fully cycles with fresh air every three to four minutes. When pressurized, a person is roughly equivalent to being at a depth of nine feet under water or diving to the bottom of the deep end of an average-sized pool. This can cause minor ear pain but ruptures are extremely rare.

Inside, a mattress and pillow support the occupant and several windows serve the dual purpose of allowing them to view the outside world as well as let light in. It is not recommended for anyone suffering from severe claustrophobia to use this type of therapy since they can feel somewhat confined.

One to two persons, depending on the chamber capacity, can lie down comfortably inside when it is fully inflated. The 'skin' resembles thick polyvinyl chloride (PVC) or hypalon material, similar to the type of composite material used in the construction of puncture resistant inflatable boats. Oxygen is piped into a mask that the occupant wears while inside the cigar shaped structure. Two heavy-gauge zippers line almost the full length of the upper portion double-insulated chamber wall, an outer one and an inner one.

Out of the Darkness

The occupant seals themselves inside and lies down placing the face mask over their mouth and nose. They first close the outer zipper, then the inner one making sure the seal is secure. Any opening in the chamber walls or closure areas, no matter how small, could rupture the unit while under pressure, rendering it useless.

When everything appears complete, a second person outside the chamber turns on the external compressor. For home use, a remote device can turn the compressor on from inside the chamber as well if there is no second person available to do so manually.

A dial, located above and behind the occupant's head, displays the pressure, which maxes out at four pounds per square inch on most home-use models. This is equivalent to being at eleven feet below sea level. This level is reached over a five, to ten minute duration depending on how quickly the occupant manually closes the pressure valve inside the chamber. It is recommended to equalize the pressure gradually by turning the valve slowly over the recommended timeframe. Closing the valve too quickly can potentially cause the occupant's eardrums to rupture from the dramatic sudden increase in pressurization.

The oxygen being consumed through the mask is seventy-five to ninety-five percent enriched oxygen. Carbon dioxide waste, naturally expelled by the occupant, is removed from the unit through two separate scrubbing vents.

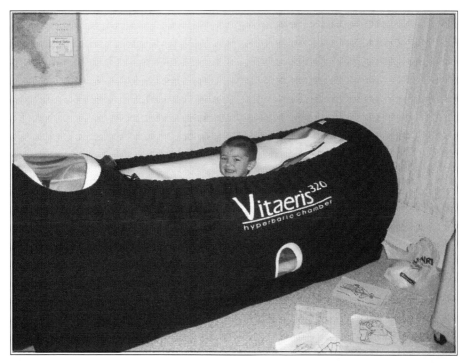

Matthew getting used to the chamber. Making it an adventure for him really helped quell his fears.

The constant hum of the compressor can be heard while the device is operating and that, as well as the popping of the occupant's ears, gives a similar sensation to flying at high altitude.

Something else rather noticeable is that the chamber also becomes uncomfortably warm, usually topping out fifteen to twenty degrees higher than the air in the surrounding room. Cooling fans and portable air conditioners placed near the compressor intake vent, located on the outside of the unit, can help cool the inside and make the experience more comfortable.

Once the chamber is fully pressurized, the occupant can then do whatever they want from reading, to using portable electronic devices, to falling asleep.

The Power of HBOT

Healthy, oxygenated blood is vital to cellular regeneration and maintenance. The increased oxygen consumption saturates the occupant's plasma, the opaque fluid that blood cells travel through, while the extra pressure forces it deeper into the body's cells and tissues. Since the oxygen is infused with the body's plasma, it can travel places too small for blood cells to reach.

Oxygen is very important to the body. It feeds and heals cells as well as carries toxins and wastes out of one's system. An increase in oxygen helps the body, in this case, to heal itself much more quickly than it normally would, especially in areas deficient in the vital gas.

Hyperbaric therapy also breaks through the blood/brain barrier, the membrane separating the tissue of the brain from the surrounding bloodstream. The barrier is akin to a sieve, only allowing those substances necessary for brain function to pass through. By adding increased pressure, inflammation in the brain – a major characteristic of autism – can be lessened.

Single Photon Emission Computed Tomography, or SPECT Scans, used mainly to provide highly detailed views of blood flow through veins and arteries in the brain showed HBOT could be helping. They displayed greatly increased blood flow, also known as hyper-profusion, to sensitive, oxygen deficient regions in the brain, over the course of several HBOT sessions.[xxi]

The device has, in fact, already been FDA approved for use in treatment of over fourteen different conditions including:
- carbon monoxide poisoning
- cyanide poisoning
- altitude / decompression sickness
- anemia
- crush injury
- actinomycosis
- clostridial myonecrosis (gas gangrene)
- diabetic wounds
- tissue infections

71

- osteomyelitis
- osteoradionecrosis (radiation tissue damage)
- skin graft trauma
- thermal burns

It has been used to treat numerous ailments and conditions as well, including:

- aids
- allergies / asthma
- atherosclerosis
- attention deficit disorder
- autism
- amyotrophic lateral sclerosis (ALS)
- Alzheimer's
- Bells Palsy
- Brain Injury
- Cancer
- Cerebral Palsy
- Chronic Fatigue Immune Dysfunction
- Coma
- Cosmetic Surgery
- Crohn's disease
- Dementia
- Depression
- diabetes
- Encephalopathy – brain injury
- Epidermal burns
- Epilepsy / Seizures
- Fibromyalgia
- Hearing Loss
- Heart Disease
- Hepatitis
- Infection
- Interstitial Cystitis
- Lupus
- Lyme Disease
- Macular Degeneration
- Memory loss

- Menopause Symptoms
- Migraines
- Multiple Chemical Sensitivity
- multiple sclerosis
- near drowning
- neuropathy
- ocular conditions
- orthopedic – musculoskeletal conditions
- Osteoporosis – decreases in bone mineral density
- Parkinson's
- Polio
- Reflex Sympathetic Dystrophy
- Rheumatic Diseases – including arthritis
- seizures
- Spinal Cord Injuries
- sports injuries
- stroke
- general wounds. [10xxii]

While its use has been well established in the medical community for treating wounds and the like for many years, research on its effectiveness to recover from autism or neurological disorders has not been conducted until recently.

---

10 For a complete list of FDA approved conditions and their definitions that HBOT can help with, please see Appendix A.

A Miracle

While driving home from the second treatment Ruth received a call from Daniel that changed her entire outlook. Her son asked from the backseat to talk to his father. He was speaking in full sentences for the first time in his life. It made her so happy she couldn't help but cry.

Something else their son began doing was craving chocolate ice cream. His parent's thought this odd since he had never shown any interest in it before. Daniel went out and bought him some, overjoyed that his son was finally talking in sentences to them.

Matthew began speaking more and more as if a fog had been lifted from him. He frequently shouted out 'look at me, look at me' to get their attention. Daniel and Ruth began brainstorming as to how they could afford to continue the treatments.

Dr. Rossignol recommended the standard series of forty dives. In hyperbaric jargon, a dive is a single chamber therapy session. After Matthew's two weeks were finished, his parents stopped HBOT therapy in favor of securing financing for a unit of their own.

After HBOT therapy, the old Matthew begins
to shine through again.

75

Daniel and Ruth inquired about other less expensive options to continuing treatments and discovered the clinic had set up a soft chamber rental program. Rossignol's patients could take the portable units and use them in the convenience of their own homes, unsupervised. This would definitely help Daniel and Ruth avoid the daily four hour trip.

A requirement the clinic had with all patients opting for this method of treatment was to have the caregivers finish a mandatory instruction class before they could rent a unit. After weighing the pros and cons, they decided not to rent.

Two months after his last hyperbaric treatment, Matthew stopped craving chocolate ice cream. Daniel and Ruth worried that some of the progress he had made might gradually slip away as well.

Matthew's parents researched side-effects of long-term HBOT use. They had read that possible complications could range from:

- pain or slight discomfort - due to increased pressure in the ear canals (known as barotraumas)
- physical injury - to the tissues of the body, surrounding cavities of air, due to moving to or from a high pressure environment)
- visual blurring – a rare occurrence that could hinder eyesight and possibly not abate for several weeks.[xxiii]

They learned that these were not issues with soft chambers since the pressures involved never reached levels that could cause these types of injuries. According to the U.S. Navy's dive tables, a person can live indefinitely at 1.3 atmospheres. That's the pressure their son would be subjected to for two hours each day.

Oxygen toxicity weighed more heavily on their minds though. Toxicity due to flooding too much oxygen into the body without allowing it to diffuse properly could potentially lead to coma or in very rare instances possibly even death. Most of the cases they had read about were very extreme and uncommon, usually the result of some other underlying issue or improper and excessive use. As long as they closely monitored their son's exposure in the chamber, they felt they had very little to worry about.

They would also set up his therapy to skip every other month. He would do a full month of treatments in the chamber followed by a resting period of equal amount. This would allow his body the time it needed to recover and naturally lower the oxygen levels within his blood back to pre-chamber parameters. This was suggested to them by Dr. Rossingol and was standard protocol at his clinic.

Once their concerns were eased, they settled on a California HBOT company by the name of OxyHealth. The company specialized in the manufacture and distribution of safe, low pressure, portable oxygen chambers for home and road use.[11]

---

11 Learn more about OxyHealth LLC from their website. http://www.oxyhealth.com/index.html

A Key in the Lock

Daniel and Ruth were excited to begin treatments. When the unit finally arrived, during the last week of February 2007, Matthew had a cold and had to wait for two weeks. Using the chamber while sick was not recommended due to the possibility of injury. Their son might experience excruciating pain in his sinuses, nose, ears and so forth.

After he was finally over his cold, Matthew began chamber therapy at home. They started slowly, with five day a week, one hour sessions. Once his parents were confident with the results, they doubled his sessions. After his first home treatment, he began craving chocolate ice cream again.

As time went by his sentence speaking increased and became more in line with what was expected for his age. He grew calmer, his hyperactivity fading to acceptable levels. He started playing with other kids and waiting his turn. His teacher noticed him much more social and less introverted. She gave him the nickname of Mr. Social. He understood more complex directions such as retrieving items for his parents based solely on their verbal directions and his vocabulary increased daily. On his fourth day of treatments, Matthew came home from school with his daily report. It was glowing.

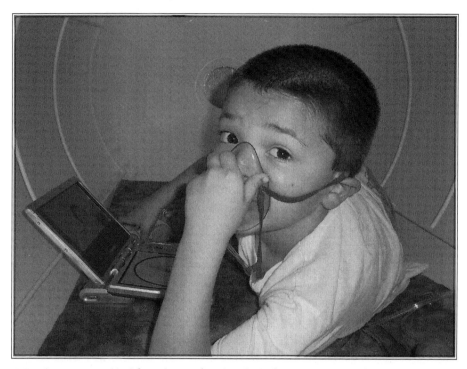

Matthew rests inside a hyperbaric chamber. Oxygen delivered via a mask can increase O$_2$ in the body by 30 to 35 percent.

The teacher wrote that he was doing great and that it had been his best day yet. This continued for the next few weeks, each report he brought home was better than the last.

Then one day Daniel and Ruth read the daily report and were shocked. The teacher wrote that their son had come into class in the morning, walked up to each kid and said their name and hello to them. The teacher was astonished, having never seen such behavior from Matthew, and finished the note with the recommendation that whatever Daniel and Ruth were doing, they should keep it up because it was working so well.

They were eager to share the specifics of their treatment methods with his teacher but in the end decided not to. They didn't want a backlash similar to what had happened to them at Matthew's previous school. They waited until the end of the school year before revealing it to her. She was very happy and excited for them since she had witnessed firsthand how their son had benefited over the course of the school year. It pleased them that someone wasn't being judgmental of what they were trying to do.

Daniel began entering the chamber himself as well, spending his time inside to rest or sleep. After a month's worth of treatments, his back, which had chronically hurt for years due to an old weightlifting injury, stopped aching. His knee, damaged from years of strain on the job, and the fact that he was slightly bow-legged, was healed to the point that he didn't need to wear his knee brace. It had become a common fixture on his leg in the last few years and he was glad to get rid of it.

A benefit Ruth received from entering the chamber with her son was that her migraines disappeared. She had hoped it would help alleviate the severe and constant pain in her chest caused by radiation therapy, but it didn't. She spent much of her time resting from the pain and it severely limited her functionality and range of motion. She was glad to be rid of the migraines at least.

Matthew was re-evaluated in May of 2007 by his school. They reversed what Shands had said and noted on his record that he had high functioning autism. They were surprised that an autism classification had been removed from his record in the first place.

The reasoning this time was that even though he was unusually affectionate for an autism case, he still exhibited far too many autistic traits to not be considered as having some form of autism or autism-like condition.

Nothing Happens
by Chance

"You should accept your child the way God made him."

"God didn't make our child this way, he didn't make Ruth have cancer, human-kind did this by polluting our planet, poisoning our food, corrupting our air supply. These are the consequences of those actions. This is what some people's bodies are telling us. God didn't do this to any child. We're doing it to ourselves. But thank God, God gives us the knowledge to correct it. To clean out our bodies, get the therapy we need. If the naysayer had cancer, wouldn't they go through chemotherapy?"
- Daniel Faiella

Ruth started a blog page on the internet at http://www.recoveringmatthew. blogspot.com regarding her son's condition and journey. She kept it private at first, only wanting some kind of journal so she could log Matthew's progress for herself and Daniel. As time went on she made it public and it grew into a way for her to inform others of her son's challenges and possibly gain valuable information and insight from those whose own children were in similar situations.

Creating the site would turn into both a blessing and a curse. It would become a place where Daniel and Ruth would receive incredible encouragement, treatment ideas from total strangers and correspondence and support from other families. The unfortunate downside was they would regularly receive vicious hate mail and accusations of neglect and harm as well as physical threats.

Time seemed to pass quickly and before they knew it, the 2007-2008 school year had begun. Matthew was almost seven years old. Along with the new year came a new teacher for Matthew to get used to. To Daniel and Ruth she seemed good but didn't appear as enthusiastic as his last teacher had been.

After several weeks, Daniel and Ruth came to the conclusion that she wasn't challenging their son enough. She didn't provide them with progress reports or their son with homework as his last teacher had done. Concerned, Daniel asked for a parent / teacher conference and voiced his observations but nothing seemed to change. After a few more frustrating weeks, Matthew's parents decided it was time to find him yet another school. They continued to send him to his current one until a better environment for him to learn in could be located.

One day, while driving around on errands, Ruth noticed a sign in front of the local YMCA. They were promoting a membership campaign and offering a free week of using the facilities with every membership sign up. Ruth asked Daniel to stop so they could try it out. She was sure Matthew would love it to the point that it would be difficult to get him out of the pool everyday. After signing up, Ruth took Matthew to the pool every day and he enjoyed it as much as she thought he would.

He had always loved swimming and getting into the water. The week flew by. On the last day Daniel was off from work and decided to join them. During the day, Ruth noticed a mother with two small children, roughly Mathew's age, in the water. Matthew kept swimming over to them saying

"Hi, little boy. Hi, little girl."

He would crowd their space, visibly upsetting the children. Daniel went to the mother and apologized for his son's intrusiveness. He explained that Matthew was autistic and that he meant no harm. That was simply how he communicated with others. He didn't know what boundaries were.

The mother told them she didn't mind at all and was extremely amazed with Matthew's speaking ability. She explained that her own son, who was a year younger than Matthew, spoke no words at all. He had been diagnosed autistic as well. Daniel, excited to meet someone else in a similar situation, began talking about hyperbaric therapy.

The mother was intrigued and told Daniel and Ruth about the school her son was in. Not only did it specialize in teaching autistic children, but placed them in a regular classroom for a portion of the day with a personal aide at their side. They could interact with children, not afflicted with the condition, in a real-world learning environment. Daniel and Ruth felt that it was just what they had been searching for and thanked her.

They had heard about the facility before but had been told by their current school that it was strictly for severe autistic cases and that their son wouldn't qualify. They later found out that wasn't true. They called up the school to arrange a meeting.

When they discovered it was only two miles away from where they currently had Matthew enrolled, they excitedly filled out the necessary paperwork to have him transferred over.

As soon as they could, Daniel and Ruth enrolled their son in the new school. They were pleased to discover classes were small. They averaged only about eleven kids to a teacher along with two additional aides in each room for supplemental support. Matthew was soon following regular classroom curricula and his parents were excited to see him begin progressing again. He ended up with the same class and teacher as the little boy he had met at the pool. The chance meeting at the YMCA had unexpectedly opened another door for the Faiella family.

For approximately an hour each day, Matthew and his personal aide would join a classroom of first graders without disabilities. He could interact and learn with them, promoting in him social skills and fostering relationships. He wasn't just stuck in a corner and forgotten about as he had been at previous institutions. He was openly encouraged to participate during classroom objectives and if teased by the other kids, would have his aide with him for support. She would also assist in keeping him focused on his current task at hand whatever that might be.

One issue he always had difficulty with was the concept of personal space. Not able to express himself in other ways, he would suddenly hug a classmate or get extremely close to them reaching out to touch their hair or clothes from time to time.

This was not always met with the innocence with which it was intended. When he would do this to his autistic friend from the pool, that boy would bite him, having no other way of showing his disapproval. Because of Matthew's intolerance to pain, he could not equate biting as painful and would not stop breaking the boy's personal space. Matthew was finally placed in another classroom to alleviate this.

His next teacher was great with him. She expected more out of him and he responded with terrific results. She began sending math and spelling work home with him for review the following day. This teacher was treating him like a student, more so than any other teacher, and this thrilled his parents. He wasn't just being watched in some sort of daycare. He was learning, not just for a small portion of the day but his entire time in class, and enjoying it.

Generation Rescue

Daniel and Ruth felt it very important to share any information they received, either through their own research or observation with their own son, with as many others as possible. They had felt overwhelmed when they began their journey since there was so much information and much more misinformation available to parents. They were excited by what their son had accomplished and they wanted others to see the progress he had made and that recovery was a viable option.

Ruth updated her blog regularly, jotting down key observations witnessed in her son's behavior. Daniel sent emails to everyone he could think of detailing new therapies and protocols that he had researched. One of his emails, regarding hyperbarics, reached the inbox of a person by the name of J.B. Handley. J.B.'s own son had been stricken with autism soon after a vaccination. The Handley's co-founded an internet site in 2005.

Named Generation Rescue (www.generationrescue.org), it was developed as a way to foster communication among parents and caregivers of autistic children. This would inform parents of recovery and to see it as a possibility. The second purpose was to let parents know they have control to amend their children's vaccination schedules. By removing unnecessary vaccines and staggering others, no child would have to endure what has become the current norm, a total exposure of up to six viruses in a single visit.

Parents could know it was all right to question their children receiving shots while they were on antibiotics or when they were already weakened from fighting some current sickness. For many children, shots are administered regardless of the above conditions. These were issues both J.B. and his wife had not known about or even felt they had power to control until after tragedy had struck their own family.

Since the beginning of their journey, J.B. and his wife had both seen remarkable progress in their own son by implementing therapies other families had tried. They saw a need for a single source of treatment options and support, knowing that parents of newly diagnosed children would only want to know what to do to help their kids. A site like this didn't exist.

Theirs would save caregivers countless hours of valuable time in trying to recover their children.

An added, and unforeseen, benefit of the site had been the creation of what has grown into a huge autism support network called the Rescue Angel network. This group of parent volunteers from all over the world, assists parents of newly diagnosed children with support and treatment ideas that have worked for their own kids. The number of angels has swelled to well over a thousand as of 2008 and they have helped over twenty-five thousand families begin down the path of recovery.

Another Piece of the Puzzle

Even though things were good, Daniel and Ruth were always concerned that Matthew wasn't progressing fast enough. They believed that there was a 'window of opportunity' that they had with him and every day that went by meant the window was closing. Daniel constantly looked for ways to help his son.

Near the beginning of his evening shift at the hotel, Daniel walked through the somewhat vacant front lobby on his way to his station. A car pulled up and he needed to be ready to assist the guests with their luggage. He adjusted his uniform. He watched the family as they exited the car. Their son seemed to display characteristics similar to those he had witnessed with his own such as stemming and looking to the side. The conversation turned toward autism.

"Someone you know have autism?"

"Yes ma'am. My son is autistic."

"So is ours." She motioned toward her young child.

The father moved toward the trunk, opening it. Daniel began placing their bags on a nearby luggage trolley. A sudden excitement filled him. "If you don't mind me asking, have you tried DAN therapies with him?"

The mother and father looked at him puzzled. "We've never heard of that. What is it?" she asked.

"We've done vitamin, nutritional and speech therapy with our son but our biggest success has come from hyperbaric oxygen therapy." He finished removing their bags.

"Our pediatrician has never mentioned any of those to us. What progress have you seen?" Both parents listened intently.

Daniel spent the trip up to their room explaining all the wonderful breakthroughs his son had made. By the time he had unloaded their bags, they were asking him how they could find out more. His enthusiasm had rubbed off on them.

They were eager to try some of the therapies with their own son who hadn't seemed to make much progress since his diagnosis. Daniel gave them Ruth's phone number so they could talk to her as well if they wished. He would continue this scenario anytime someone inquired of him.

Over several months many parents called back to tell Ruth of their wonderful progress. Their own children appeared to be benefiting greatly. Both Daniel and Ruth were pleased that other children were recovering in some small way due to what they had discovered on their journey with their own child.

One day, while working overtime during a large hotel conference, Daniel checked a family's bags and noticed the young daughter confined to a wheelchair. The girl's mother explained her daughter had cerebral palsy and was unable to go anywhere without the chair. Daniel asked her if she had ever heard of hyperbaric therapy. During his research, he had discovered that one of the things it was being used to help alleviate was cerebral palsy symptoms.

The mother replied that she had heard of it but admitted they hadn't tried it yet. Daniel told her how it had helped his own son and she was astonished. The topic changed direction and she asked Daniel if he had heard about adult stem cell therapy. He hadn't and thought that stem cells were banned.

The mother mentioned that while it was true that the harvesting of embryonic stem cells was highly controversial, the same didn't hold true for adult stem cells.

An embryonic stem cell, since it is still not fully developed, has the ability to 'grow' into any other type of cell. Introducing these types of stem cells into a region can be potentially dangerous since the cell has the ability to grow into a cell not needed and/or possibly harmful to the surrounding tissues. There were also ethical issues surrounding how these types of cells were harvested.

Some studies utilizing these cells had inconclusive or adverse reactions on those individuals undergoing trails with them. Reactions varied such as severe inflammation due to the recipient's own immune system attacking the cells as intruders after identifying them as foreign, the cells growing into cells not needed or harmful to the area they were introduced such as hair cells growing inside the brain as well as many other similar incidents.

Unlike embryonic stem cell therapy, there were no known side-effects associated with adult stem cells. Doctors had been ethically extracting them from cord blood since 1940 and injection trials in humans had been studied for decades.[xxiv]

Adult stem cell therapy had shown considerable promise, was a natural process in the body and was already FDA approved as a treatment for over seventy-three different diseases and disorders. Some people claiming that the form of treatment had cured them of their ailments fully.

An adult stem cell is a special type of cell that is already fully grown, with the ability to regenerate or maintain the cells and tissues that it is located in. It also contains no visible traits, unlike specialized cells, yet is found among them throughout the body. Since it is already fully mature, there is no danger of it 'growing' into some other type of cell not needed by the region in which it is located and thus causing complications.[xxv] This is different from what sometimes occurs in embryonic stem cell therapy. There are no currently known methods to force embryonic stem cells to grow into specific cells with a hundred percent certainty. Adult stem cells can be extracted without ethical dilemma and a person can even have their own cells reinserted into problem areas in their own body.

Because of this huge difference between the two types of stem cells, countries such as China have been spending large amounts of resources on researching adult stem cells. Their potential had been documented for some years now and they are known or thought to cure or alleviate a multitude of diseases / disorders.

The mother of the child with cerebral palsy admitted that she had entertained the idea of traveling to China to have the procedure performed on her own child. At over twenty thousand dollars for the treatment alone not to mention flight and lodging however, it was well out of her budget. She mentioned that she could provide Daniel with more information regarding the procedures involved if he left her his contact information.

Daniel eagerly offered his personal email address to her. When he got home at the end of his shift, he told Ruth about what he had learned and in an instant was researching to find out more about this new discovery. He located a handful of clinics, all outside the United States, offering either embryonic or adult stem cell therapy to alleviate or cure a host of various disorders and conditions. After more digging, much to his discontent, he came to the conclusion that many of these clinics were making highly exaggerated claims probably just to profit off others pain.

One in Mexico had even been implicated in a rather embarrassing scandal in which it had been exposed as having injected its patients with adult stem cells from cows instead of human donors.

A hospital in Ukraine, a country that in recent years has had an explosion in the export business of stem cells, had come under criminal investigation after several apparently healthy new-born babies had died soon after birth for no apparent reason. One chilling claim was that the baby's bodies were dismembered to allow easy harvesting of bone marrow stem cells. The infants were then presumably discarded, buried in the hospital's own cemetery.[xxvi]

Stories such as these and many more, alarmed and frightened Daniel as to what harm could befall his son. Matthew was counting on him and he couldn't let him down. Questions still clouded his mind, no matter what he read. What if the treatments harmed his son? What if they made his condition worse? What if they killed him? Each question pushed closer and closer to the front of his thoughts.

He spent long hours following study after study. He read about a person stricken with lupus who after stem cell therapy saw a dramatic reversal of their symptoms. Another, suffering from scleroderma[12] was able to fully function again with stem cells. And a man with multiple sclerosis who celebrated being MS free for five years in 2008 after stem cells. [13] [xxvii] The lists of success stories just kept growing.

He kept researching until one promising facility, in Costa Rica, finally did catch his eye. Its website mentioned that it had used adult stem cells to treat:

- Autoimmune diseases
- Cerebral Palsy
- Diabetes Type 2
- Heart Failure
- Multiple Sclerosis
- Osteoarthritis
- Parkinson's
- Rheumatoid Arthritis
- Stroke.[14]

It appeared credible by all accounts and had a substantial and very pleased list of past patients from all over the world reporting great strides in all kinds of diseases and disorders. It had several reputable doctors on staff – many with medical certificates and honors received both in the United States as well as Costa Rica.

---

12 A condition in which the organs of the body grow hard and thick.

13 Learn of more stem cell success stories at http://www.frc.org/insight/adult-stem-cell-sucess-stories-2008-jan-june

14 The Costa Rican stem cell clinic's website is located at http://www.cellmedicine.com

Stem Cells

Daniel scoured the web, locating a peer review paper detailing other autistic children that had gone through adult stem cell trails. It was published in the Journal of Translational Medicine and titled <u>Stem Cell Therapy for Autism</u>. The results of the study were enlightening and highly promising.[15][xxviii]

He located individuals who had the treatment for various conditions and contacted them directly to learn as much as he could about their stories. Everyone he contacted only had praise for the treatment and what it had done for them.

He discovered a family in Miami who had traveled to Costa Rica to help their autistic daughter. They had been the first in the world to go public with the astonishing progress she had made. Her behavior changes, soon after her first week of treatments, were nothing short of remarkable.

Daniel attempted to contact the family with his questions. As fate would have it, they had already booked a night at a popular local hotel. Daniel was thrilled to learn it was the one he worked at. He greeted them when they arrived and he spent some time meeting their daughter and learning of their journey first-hand. The more he listened, the more he became convinced that he needed to do the same thing for his own son.

Hungry for more information on stem cells, he continued to search locating a startling account. Doctors had injected adult stem cells into a sixteen year old boy who had accidentally been shot in the heart with a nail gun. The front wall of the boy's heart had been shredded. Stem cells had been harvested from the teenager's own bone marrow in a first of its kind spontaneous clinical trial. The heart sealed itself as stem cells eventually repaired all the damage.[xxix]

---

15 A transcript of the study, as of 2008, can be found at http://www.translational-medicine.com/content/pdf/1479-5876-5-30.pdf

Out of the Darkness

In several animal studies, adult stem cells showed promise as they, time and again, sought out areas of damage and transformed them, repairing as needed. By injecting a concentration of them into a damaged area, the body could heal at a more substantial rate.

Finding a Compatible Match

Daniel contacted the Costa Rican clinic. They provided answers to all his questions. The stem cell introduction process, according to the clinic, was actually quite simple. Adult stem cells are harvested from umbilical cord blood after birth. They are not extracted from fetuses so there is nothing unethical about harvesting them. Most umbilical cord biomaterial today is thrown away. It's disposed of in thick, sealable bio-waste bags before being hauled off to the incinerator.

Everyone has a number of stem cells in their body at any given point in their life. The amount varies depending on things such as genetic makeup and age. Older people have less of these cells than do young people. These adult stem cells are vital to many functions in the body, chief among them being the healing of tissues and organs. This is why a child heals from a cut much faster than someone much older with an identical injury. The child's body is flooded with stem cells, constantly revitalizing their young system.

The cells are collected from donor materials and, when the recipient is ready, injected directly into the bloodstream via the arm. Stem cells immediately begin healing any damage they encounter as well as reducing inflammation. They travel throughout the body seeking out areas in which they may be needed. Homing in on injured areas that produce specific proteins indicating the area is damaged, adult stem cells begin to rebuild.

In order to lessen the possibility of rejection, the doctors look for signs of cellular immunity. If a patient's body attacks the donated cells, there is the potential for serious and unnecessary complications. The patient's own blood is extracted beforehand and typed against a series of different potential donor stem cell lines. This allows the doctors to witness which batches of stem cells are more easily compatible with the patient's own blood while still outside the body.

The cultures are allowed to mix for up to twenty-four hours. Any negative reactions will occur within that time-frame. Because of this method, the patient's risk is minimized and no immune system suppression medication is necessary. Infection risks due to rejection are virtually non-existent.

Daniel was assured by the clinic that International blood screening standards were implemented against all possible donor blood samples. All donated blood was thoroughly screened to see if it contained antibodies for Syphilis, HIV, Hepatitis B, Hepatitis C and Anti HTLV virus among other diseases before being allowed into the donor pool.

Since the cells travel throughout the body helping as necessary, injecting them directly into the brain – in the case of autism – is not necessary. It had been previously proven that under normal conditions, stem cells can cross the blood / brain barrier without harm.

The cells can be injected into the spine for quicker access to the brain via the spinal fluid 'highway'. This has not been tested in children ten years or younger due to possible complications that could potentially arise given their smaller stature. Daniel believed a combination of stem cell and hyperbaric therapy might be the solution needed to help unlock his son.

Against the Odds

The clinic was using two separate types of adult stem cells to attack autism from a couple of different directions simultaneously.

Mesenchymal (MSCs) stem cells, derived from umbilical cord blood, placentas, bone marrow and adipose tissue (fat cells) had been proven effective in the treatment of acute ischemic heart disease among other conditions. They were able to assist in the restoration of other cells such as smooth muscle and endothelial cells. MSCs could aid in the production of cartilage, fat, bone, tendons and muscle. These types of cells also had the ability to create increased oxygen, repair the heart, bone cartilage and bone as well as build other connective tissue cells.[xxx] They also have been documented to decrease inflammation.

CD34 hematopoietic stem cells are another type of cell harvested from umbilical cord blood and bone marrow that can assist in curing digestive disorders as well as boosting weakened immune systems.[xxxi] Hematopoietic means producing new blood vessels. CD34 cells are believed to:

- stimulate the generation of new blood vessels in tissues deprived of oxygen
- provide increased blood flow in the temporal region of the brain, an area believed to be oxygen depleted in autistic children
- assist in the recovery of post myocardial infarction (heart failure)
- alleviate end stage angina
- alleviate peripheral artery disease
- prevent stroke
- stop liver failure

Focusing on the digestive tract in autism patients seems a logical choice since many have what is known as 'leaky gut' syndrome. Their digestive system doesn't function properly and many nutrients normally gleaned by the body are missed, passing right through their system. This can lead to symptoms similar to Crone's disease such as weight loss, vomiting, abdominal pain and diarrhea.

Hematopoietic stem cells are currently in Phase III clinical trials in the U.S. for Crone's disease and are showing favorable results in combating it.[xxxii] This helped shed light on why supplements had been successful for Matthew. They were re-supplying his body with nutrients it was unable to process naturally.

There is a faction of doctors that believe autism begins in the digestive system with symptoms in the brain occurring due to a trickle-down effect. They believe that since the body is not able to process the nutrients the brain needs, the brain suffers for it. So while the effects are noticed in brain function, the underlying root cause begins in the digestive tract. It is important to note that not all autism specialists believe this hypothesis.

Daniel felt his son's main issue was hyper-profusion – not receiving enough blood and oxygen to his brain – so he and Ruth decided on CD34 cells only. He felt that his son's brain was starving and had been improving with hyperbaric therapy because it was saturated in oxygen. CD34 cells could potentially create more oxygen at a higher rate than the hyperbaric therapy could alone.

Discussing their findings for weeks, Daniel and Ruth contacted the clinic via email correspondence and by telephone several times with questions and concerns. The clinic was fine with their request to only introduce CD34 cells to their son. They finally decided to go with the Costa Rican medical facility.

Realizing that although adult stem cells showed much promise, they shouldn't be considered a "magic pill" capable of curing their child. They began the process to get their son on the admission list for stem cell injections. They had been told that they might not see any visible difference in their son until six months after the treatment.

They also opted to take Matthew off his other treatments such as chelation and diet modifications during cell therapy. They didn't want to run the risk of killing the newly introduced cells. HBOT therapy was halted as well. Matthew's doctor suggested he not begin it again until three months after his return from Costa Rica.

Daniel began calling autism help organizations such as Autism Speaks and Autism One to continue to get the word out about the things helping his son. He received little response from any of the organizations he contacted. Ruth kept her blog up to date. For every word of encouragement they received, they were hit with several other messages of anger, outrage and discouragement.

Many of the naysayers had vicious and mean things to say to them. People would tell them they were horrible parents. That filling others' minds with false hope and subjecting their own child to untested practices and useless, possibly dangerous procedures was in fact hurting him far more than helping.

Daniel defended their position frequently, citing all the research they had conducted before proceeding with any treatment. He wrote back to everyone that questioned them. Most of his correspondence was usually met with more close-minded vulgar and hateful responses, if any at all.

Parents of autistic children, that had been their friends before, began talking badly about them. This shocked and hurt them both but it didn't stop them.

Daniel contacted local news affiliates in an attempt to see if they wanted to do a story on his son. When normal inquiries didn't work as he had expected, he mentioned to them that something historic was going to happen and asked if they would like to be a part of history or watch it instead. One television station finally called him back and after several emails and phone calls, set up an interview.

The night before the interview, Daniel received a call from someone representing a large non-profit autism assistance organization. The caller, hearing what they were attempting, put a lot of fear into Daniel. The person urged him to not go through with his plan for Matthew, citing that it was untested and could possibly hurt or kill his son.

He thanked the man for his concern then explained his position. He wasn't jumping in blind. He cared deeply for his son's well-being and had researched the procedures extensively. By the end of the call the person was more enlightened but said that unfortunately their organization couldn't support Daniel publicly. Since there was still so much misconception, the organization was afraid to be associated with the procedure. The caller wished him good luck.

The call had been a test of Daniel's resolve. After faltering a bit and canceling the next day's interview because of the fear and doubt the caller had placed in his mind, he decided that he was doing the right thing by going forward. He called the clinic as a final check to make sure it would be okay for him to go public, then contacted the television station to reschedule the interview during the following week.

On Sunday February 24th, 2008, the family boarded an international flight to Costa Rica. It was early in the morning and they would be stopping for a two and a half hour layover in Miami before flying on for another three hours. They were looking forward to the journey and after all their research had high hopes their son would be helped by the cells. They were anxious yet hopeful that what they were about to do would open up the world for their son. Matthew was seven years old.

Costa Rica

On Monday morning they left their hotel having not eaten breakfast, catching the provided van to go straight to the clinic. As part of the clinic protocol, Matthew was restricted from eating at least eight hours prior to having his blood extracted for compatibility testing. Since he couldn't eat anything Daniel and Ruth decided not to as well. The temperature in San José was mild and comfortable.

They took in the sights and sounds of the city on their drive to the clinic. The quaint streets, narrow by American standards were lined with small homes, each one a different color from the last. They watched locals pick through the morning's produce, native fruits and vegetables that they had never seen before, along side-street open-air markets. Some vendors carried bushels of fruit into the busy intersections during red lights in hopes of making a sale or two from a passing motorist.

They could see the peaks of a few of the volcanoes bordering the city in the distance. One smoldered slightly as they watched it from the back of the van. Their hotel concierge had told them that they should take the tour to the Poás volcano before leaving.

Matthew stared out the window past the buildings and up into the lush greenery of the surrounding mountains. The lower portions of the mountains were covered in tropical trees and vegetation. This was definitely not like Florida. Daniel and Ruth had been so excited about the procedure for their son that they hadn't considered what they could see and do in the country afterward. The nice, simple homes soon gave way to large, modern office-buildings as they continued down the streets of the capital city.

Their van finally rounded a corner reaching the front of the clinic. The structure looked like a small, ordinary office building nestled on the corner intersection of two small streets. There was a single driveway leading up to the front.

They got out of the van and entered the building. Inside was larger than the outside made it appear and the walls were painted in nice, warm colors. The posh waiting room in front of them contained three over-sized sofas and a salt-water aquarium in one of the walls.

They checked in, asking many questions of the knowledgeable and courteous staff. All their inquiries were answered to their satisfaction and, after filling out several forms, they were ushered into an examining room.

Ruth reassured Matthew that it would be over soon. Like most children, he didn't like needles. They continued asking the same questions again and again to be absolutely sure of what was happening and were given adequate answers each time. The doctors, nurses and staff were extremely patient, knowledgeable and understanding with them.

The staff gave Ruth a green patient gown for Matthew to wear. It would allow easier access to the brace support they were going to add to his arm. He looked like a doctor in it and Daniel and Ruth told him how proud they were of him. They called him doctor and he enjoyed imagining himself as such.

The doctors sedated Matthew with nitrous oxide and inserted an intravenous catheter, two inches long, into his arm. The catheter was necessary to easily withdraw blood and administer the stem cells over the course of the week without having to keep re-sticking Matthew. It would remain in his vein, taped to his arm.

The nurses placed a brace, similar in appearance to a splint, around his arm. This would ensure that the catheter wouldn't fall out as well as keep him from removing it himself. They then withdrew six vials of blood to be tested for viruses and mixed with potential donor cell cultures. When the nitrous wore off and Matthew woke up, a half an hour later, he cried for quite a while.

"Papa, get it out, please help me."

This broke Daniel's heart but he and Ruth reassured their son that it would feel better soon. When his parents wouldn't help, he reached out to anyone walking in the hall as they passed his door. He pleaded for them to take the brace off his arm.

Another child about the same age as Matthew was undergoing the same treatment in an adjoining room. Daniel introduced them to each other.

"Look, you guys match." He said pointing to the other child's braced arm. This helped calm Matthew down. Daniel was thankful they were done. They went back to the hotel to let their son rest. They worried about what the next session, scheduled for tomorrow, might bring.

Tuesday afternoon Matthew was visibly upset to be back. His discomfort from the day before was still very fresh in his mind.

As they waited to be seen, Daniel noticed other patients at the clinic being treated for all sorts of conditions. Some had suffered strokes while others had severe rheumatoid arthritis or multiple sclerosis.

Daniel introduced himself to an older gentleman who mentioned that he was in a wheelchair the first time he came in. After stem cells, he was walking again, playing golf and doing all the things he had longed to do before but was unable to. Daniel felt better about his decision after talking with these patients and seeing the progress they had made in person. It was quite different than reading about their remarkable stories on the web.

When it came time for Matthew's injection, Daniel and Ruth comforted their son as Dr. Solano, the director of the clinic, performed the procedure.

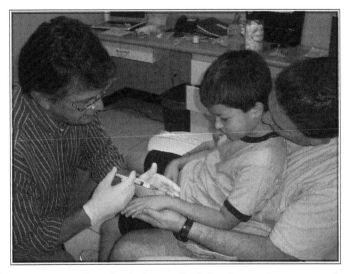

The first injection is administered. The brace is removed so that the doctor can access the port. Matthew does great.

He took a syringe of donor stem cells that had been previously typed to Matthew's blood successfully and hooked it up to the catheter, slowly emptying its contents fully.

Matthew flinched slightly, his face showing his disapproval, but he remained calm. The entire process was over in less than two minutes. After observing him for a while, the director told Daniel and Ruth that Matthew didn't need to remain in the clinic since their hotel wasn't that far away.

Out of the Darkness

This was the clinic's standard operating procedure. Clients rarely, if ever, had to stay overnight.

He told them not to hesitate to call if they noticed anything out of the ordinary such as swelling at the injection site, changes in behavior or mood or sudden fever. The clinic provided a twenty-four hour emergency number for any questions or concerns that might come up during the night as a precautionary measure. Daniel and Ruth were grateful they could take Matthew out of the clinic and get his mind off of the injection. They called a taxi and went back to the hotel.

The rest of the week followed the same scenario. By Tuesday night Ruth realized Matthew was sleeping through the night. Prior to the trip, she had stopped giving him melatonin since she didn't want any interactions between his supplements and the stem cells. He was in a strange and different place other than his home and yet was fine. It was the first time in over two and a half years he had ever slept through the night without having to take his supplement.

Matthew received identical injections on Wednesday, Thursday and Friday. His parents carefully observed his progress as each day went by; taking him out to explore the country and take his mind off things afterward.

As the week progressed, their son appeared calmer, more alert to them. He started demanding more attention from his parents instead of playing by himself or sitting alone. By the end of the week, the doctors and nurses at the clinic had even noticed marked changes in his behavior with many of the staff commenting that he appeared much more talkative and outgoing by the end of the week.

On Friday, after his last injection, the doctor removed the catheter and brace from Matthew's arm. Matthew was very happy to have it out. The family traveled back to the hotel and packed their stuff in preparation for the plane trip home the following morning. Early Saturday they boarded a flight to Miami International airport then a smaller jet to Orlando. They were exhausted but exhilarated at what they had accomplished for their son.

Autism Cured?

As the weeks passed, Daniel and Ruth noticed changes in Matthew again. Almost immediately, he was calmer, sleeping better and understanding more. He stopped wetting his bed altogether.

His teacher sent notes home stating that he was raising his hand and participating in class activities. Before they had left, the teachers in the school had been indifferent not believing stem cells would work.

A few months later, Matthew's exercise-induced asthma disappeared. Gone were the coughing fits that so often accompanied him after a good run around the playground. His understanding and reasoning abilities continued to improve.

On June 8th, the family prepared to fly back to Costa Rica for a second round of stem cell treatments. This time they knew more of what to expect and were eager to see what progress could occur. They would have to wait a little longer to see the results however. It wasn't for another two months after their return that they began noticing improvements.

Daniel wondered if the reasons for a delay this time were because it was the middle of summer and Matthew's mind wasn't being challenged by school as it had been when he got back from his first trip.

He also speculated that perhaps the first round had healed a lot of quick fix issues as the stem cells made their way through his son's body and this time they were working on deeper more isolated yet less visible areas. Both he and Ruth were not disappointed by the delay after the second trip. Matthew's decent hadn't happened overnight and it was logical that some aspects of his healing would take time.

After school started up in the fall and his brain was being challenged again, Matthew's progress jumped forward. His rapid recovery allowed him to integrate more into the regular classes with standard student curricula. His time became split down the middle with fifty percent of it being allocated to classroom study with mainstream children his age.

Matthew started counting coins, easily grasping the concept of money. He began to tell time and was able to tackle mental challenges at a much higher level than he previously could, even just before leaving on the second trip. His literacy progressed to the point that he could read at a first grade level and spell at a second grade level.

He became more outgoing, mentioning people by name and wanting to communicate and interact with them by his own choice without coaxing of any kind. Daniel and Ruth were able to take him out to places such as the movies and he would sit, watching the screen attentively the entire length of the film. A world of possibility was opening up before their son and they were thrilled for him. Gone were the days of constant running up and down aisles and tantrums at the drop of a hat.

Of the myriad of original autistic symptoms Matthew had gradually developed over the years, only stemming and echoing were still visible now and those were greatly diminished. All other autistic indicators no longer seemed present.

November of that same year, the family flew back to Costa Rica for a third treatment regime. Direct spinal injection was mentioned to them as an option this time. It would allow the cells easier and quicker access to the brain via traveling through the spinal cord rather than having to go through the smaller arteries in the arm.

After careful consideration, Daniel and Ruth opted for the original injection protocol their son had received on his two prior trips. They felt that the cells, although having to travel farther, would still reach their necessary destinations. Matthew was familiar with the original procedure and they didn't want to introduce any new stress to their son. Treatment costs would also be substantially less since an anesthesiologist, or doctor specializing in providing spinal injections, would not be necessary.

When they returned home, Daniel and Ruth noticed that while their son didn't make any huge leaps as he had the first time, he did seem to understand complex commands better. He also seemed better capable of saying things in the appropriate context.

After hyperbaric therapy, when his parents would ask if he wanted to play hide and seek, his reply would be "yes, yes, yes" however they could tell he really didn't understand what they wanted him to do. When they mentioned freeze tag, he understood it was chasing each other but couldn't grasp the concept of bases and being safe. After his third stem cell trip, he understood all of these concepts with ease and learned to apply them himself.

Silver

While following studies on the web one day, Daniel stumbled across yet another promising therapy. A health site was promoting trace amounts of silver in a medicinal grade, soluble, liquid colloidal or 'glue-like' form. Their main product was a fluid consisting of minute, slightly negatively charged, silver particles held in suspension. The site claimed that the properties within silver kept a person healthy by improving their immune system. Daniel was especially interested in silver's ability to kill yeast. He had learned that HBOT stirred up the yeast in a person's digestive system.[xxxiii] By introducing silver, he could now effectively kill it and have his son's own system remove it naturally.

It has, in fact, been used for many centuries. People in the fourteenth century knew of its effectiveness at combating disease. European nobility of the time insisted that their newborn children suck on a silver spoon as a penetrative measure against the plaque. Those with status and wealth had a lesser percentage of death than the poverty stricken masses.[xxxiv]

Doctors of the nineteenth century prescribed their patients to eat off of silver forks, spoons, knives and plates because they believed the silver in the utensils would kill off any bacteria harbored in the food. This was the birth of 'silverware'. Today's world has forgotten this and has moved to cheap ceramic and plastic eating implements which do not kill bacteria within food.

People living in remote areas would throw silver coins into their wells and drinking water to kill bacteria and make the water more potable. Containers for holding perishable liquids such as milk were formed from it to keep contents fresher, longer.

Yet another example of silver being used as a health aid began with a practice in England. The wealthy were able to produce a silver type of salt which they took internally, sometimes in very high doses. The methods some used to extract the silver from the salt were crude. This coupled with high doses had the unsettling side-effect of turning the patient's skin a brilliant shade of blue. Although there were no health risks, their skin would remain permanently blue for the rest of their lives.

Out of the Darkness

Before 1938 silver was regularly used as an antibiotic in the United States. The FDA actually recognizes it as a drug, pre 1938.[xxxv] It was only when the pharmaceutical companies began to grow, that it stopped being produced for this purpose. They replaced it with their own antibiotics.

Silver nitrate had been used as a bacterial detoxifier for years while silver iodide had been introduced into the eyes of newborn babies to prevent blindness due to bacterial contamination.

There are studies dating back to the early 1970's conducted at the State University of New York in which it was discovered that silver ions could induce fibrocytes to differentiate into stem cells and back again. Silver was actually shown to grow new stem cells.[xxxvi]

Daniel was intrigued and located several other sites that all seemed to point to the healing properties of silver. During a wellness visit he mentioned it to Matthew's pediatrician. She knew immediately what he was talking about and confirmed his thoughts of it improving the immune system.

No known biological virus has ever been able to build up a resistance to silver.[xxxvii] This is unlike pharmaceutical antibodies that over time lose their potency leading to super virus strains. Silver has been shown to kill harmful bacteria within the gut.

The silver used to heal has identical properties to the silver extracted from the ground in the production of jewelry. The difference is the amount used. The human body doesn't need much, ten parts per million is a good starting amount. Products containing this level can be found in many local health food stores although much care must be taken to research which of these companies is legitimate. Since colloidal silver is labeled as a nutritional supplement, it is not regulated by the government as drugs are.

There are methods to extract and convert silver with the use of salt water or salt extract however it is not highly recommended as doing so can lead to a condition known as argyria. This affliction occurs when silver in its elemental, sulfide or selenide form is deposited in the layer of cells under the skin, hair follicles, glands and nerves. It prompts the body to increase melatonin production and that, coupled with the accumulated silver, causes a bluish-gray discoloration to the skin.

A famous case of this condition can be seen in what happened to Paul Karason. He made his own, homemade silver extract, ingesting over two thousand parts per million a day. He had heard of silver's benefits and wanted to clear up a skin condition on his face as well as fix sinus and arthritic issues.

The silver did the job incredibly well. His arthritis, dermatitis and sinus problems were all cured. He hasn't been sick a day in his life since. His only unfortunate side-effect from taking so much silver so quickly and with his method of extraction has been for his skin to turn a brilliant shade of slate blue. There have been a couple of cases where argyria has been reversed but they are few and far between.

Mr. Karason has opted to leave his skin alone and it will remain that way for the rest of his life. These days he is called the 'blue man'. He doesn't mind the trade-off in the least. A lesser amount of silver, prepared with proper equipment and materials, can provide the same health benefits that Mr. Karason experienced without the added side-effects.[xxxviii]

Excited and secure in his research both on-line and with the family pediatrician, Daniel ordered a bottle of colloidal silver. He decided on a product called Argentyn 23. It was the only silver colloidal product certified pyrogen and endotoxin free. Pyrogen and endotoxin are both harmful to the body.[xxxix] It also was manufactured in a process ensuring purity and ideal particle dispersion and sizing.

When it arrived he began taking it, carefully monitoring any possible ill-effects. After about a month of use, he remained fully healthy while the rest of his family and friends all succumbed to the seasonal bout of flu. After they both recovered, Ruth and Matthew began taking it as well.

Daniel and Ruth witnessed a noticeable difference in Matthew's ability to have bowel movements. The silver was killing the harmful levels of yeast in his digestive system more efficiently than any medicine they had put him on previously.

Gold

While researching the properties of silver further, Daniel discovered gold. Revered as an 'elixir of the gods' by the Egyptians, they readily ingested it and used it in dentistry, feeling it helped their mental, physical and spiritual states.[xl]

The Alchemists of ancient Europe would later come to find similar beliefs in the metal. They fabricated pills coated with it and mixed minute particles in water to comfort sore limbs. In Roman times it was integrated into tonics and creams which were then applied to the body or ingested to help alleviate or heal various disorders.[xli]

At the end of the 19th century, gold suspended in water was used for treating heart ailments as well as improving circulation. Chinese villagers in some regions still place a gold coin in with their boiling rice from time to time, a tradition dating back centuries. In the early 1900's doctors began implanting pieces of gold in patients near inflamed joints. The effects of which, would usually render the pain tolerable or remove it altogether. Colloidal gold was used to treat addiction disorders such as alcoholism.

Gold never tarnishes or corrodes and is considered a super-conductor of electrical current. It is used to coat the ends of high-end electronic cable for superior reception and minimal degradation. It is completely non-toxic and so far as is currently known has no adverse interactions with any drugs.

Today, many surgical tools and devices are plated with the precious metal. Netting used to repair injured nerves, blood vessels, membranes and bones is made from it. It is used to help retard multiple cancer growth as well as target specific cells. It is a form of treatment for rheumatoid arthritis, mental / emotional health and increases mental acuity. The element has even been documented in some studies to increase I.Q. levels.[xlii]

While learning of all the remarkable properties of gold, Daniel noticed the term ionic gold continually crop up. He found out that many gold-toting products contain this form of gold which is actually a gold chloride (gold salt) and not the pure form of gold.

The reason this form is so readily available is because it is incredibly easy to manufacture. Anything made with this type of gold solution should not be ingested as it is a well-known neurotoxin to humans and can mix readily with other compounds in the body.

The pure form of gold on the other hand is inert and non-toxic to the body. Daniel discovered that it was because of this harmful type of gold solution that real colloidal gold had received a bad reputation by association.

CES and PEMF

He also became interested in brain damage cures feeling that parts of his son's brain had been injured but could recover so long as he could find the right stimulus. It wasn't long before he located some information related to Cranial Electrical Stimulation or CES and became very interested in what he was reading.

Advanced by an almost forgotten brilliant American immigrant of the early twentieth century by the name of Nicola Tesla, electrical healing has made many remarkable strides in the last century. While the mechanics of its healing power are not yet fully known, many studies have been conducted over the decades showing how CES devices have helped brain conditions such as anxiety, depression, insomnia, pain and addiction among others, lessen in their severity or, in some cases, disappear altogether.[xliii]

The therapy had already been FDA approved for over twenty-seven years. The side effects, if any, include mild dizziness, skin irritation, nausea and headaches. Several studies have been conducted that tend to suggest that electrical current generated by CES devices appear to activate clusters of nerve cells along the brainstem.

These cell groups, in turn, produce the chemicals serotonin and acetylcholine. The location of these nerve clusters is important since they act as a central hub for the rest of the nervous system, controlling electrical and chemical activity in neurological systems throughout the entire body.

They also produce alpha waves in the brain, a state associated with calmness and better mental focus. Stress and agitation, both harmful for the body, are reduced and mood is stabilized. This has shown great promise in curing anxiety, depression and sleeping disorders.

The device that caught Daniel's attention the most due to its impeccable safety record was simply called the Alpha-Stim.[xliv] An FDA approved class 2A medical device, it sends low electrical pulses to the brain.

Similar in appearance to a large portable mp3 player, the machine consists of the hand-held unit with a pair of clips connected to it via a wire. An LCD displays various readings as to what the device is currently set for. Two dials allow the user to alter the current in either of two channels, each leading to its own clip, independent of one another. A third dial allows a time for the current session to be set.

The user attaches the clips comfortably on the lobes of each ear, turns the device on, and adjusts the dials accordingly. The machine then distributes micro-current electrical pulses to the skull via the clips in the amplitude they had already pre-set for their session.

As the name implies, the Alpha-Stim stimulates and magnifies the generation of alpha waves inside the brain making a person feel completely relaxed while still in an alert state. Alpha waves are important in that they force the brain to produce endorphins which assist in pain relief and serotonin which battles depression and insomnia.

When a person's brain is producing high levels of these waves, it is easier for them to assimilate and retain new information from the world around them. People who do not have stress or brain disease have been documented to generate higher amounts of alpha waves than those with these conditions. It is an accepted form of treatment for a plethora of ailments in several countries all over the world today.

PEMF also utilizes electrical current but the energy is contained in a coil that is then placed near the body. By being in close proximity, an electrical field is emitted into the body.

Because of this, it can target any problem areas directly. Daniel was very interested in focusing on Matthew's brain and liver. He set up a protocol to administer the device three times a day, thirty minutes each session.

The first fifteen minutes the device would focus on Matthew's brain and the last fifteen minutes would be devoted to helping his liver. He had to locate a doctor working in alternative medicine to get a prescription.

Use of these devices has been shown to stimulate the fgf2 protein which aids cells in growth and repair among other things. Another benefit is that these machines have also displayed the ability to increase the amount of natural mesenchymal stem cells in the body.[xlv]

What the Future Holds

It's human nature to not become vested in something unless it affects a person or someone they care about. Most people that become autism activists do so out of necessity. They are fighting for their own children, nieces and nephews, grandkids and so forth. With the unfortunate epidemic of cases in recent years, has come a greater awareness that a major problem exists and that steps must be taken to fully identify and rectify this.

The knowledge behind what causes autism and autism related neurological disorders has come a long way from the refrigerator mom references of the 1960's. There is still a long and arduous road ahead, however and we must struggle everyday against the miles of misinformation, selfish profiteering and misguided, though well meaning, ignorance.

Before my son was diagnosed I had no idea what this condition was or how it would drastically alter not only his own life but the lives of all those that loved him. My drive to find a solution doesn't come from a deep stubbornness inside me but a determination to give my son the best possible life he can have. I've seen Matthew make incredible strides in his journey. Those who told us it was pointless to even try have fallen on the wayside time and again. Matthew has gone from reverse, to moving forward and each new day he gets faster and faster until the doubters have just become a blur in the passing scenery. In a way they are necessary. If we hadn't been told there was no hope for him, it wouldn't have lit the fire it did.

After countless hours of reading and re-reading medical papers, communicating with other parents in similar situations, phone conversations and face to face meetings with leading autism doctors I have come to the following beliefs. I feel autism, and autism related neurological disorders are caused by a number of different yet inter-related stimuli.

Some people are genetically pre-disposed to be susceptible to specific environmental triggers. These triggers can be, as in many cases, vaccines full of heavy toxic metals and harmful organisms. They can include man-made pollution in the air, water and soil, and certain types of bacterial infections, and parasites – such as those transported by ticks and other insects.

When one or more of these triggers is introduced into a genetically weakened immune system it's like lighting a match in a gas station. The body can't cope and begins to form a disconnect. The digestive system breaks down. The brain can't communicate properly. I think of it more like a rubix cube than a puzzle. There are many different sides and each turn can be more confusing than the last. You have to look at the entire cube and not just a side at a time.

Limiting certain things, such as gluten and casein, from the diet can help restore the guts original flora. Chelation, properly administered, can assist in removing toxic metals from the system allowing it to heal itself. Hyperbaric Oxygen therapy infuses the body with oxygen which is harmful to anaerobic bacteria such as those that thrive in children with these disorders. It also helps build cells, increase waste disposal and decrease inflammation. Stem cell injections introduce vast quantities of these amazing repair cells into the system to allow healing and regeneration to occur. Silver and gold kill harmful organisms dug into these children's systems not wanting to leave. CES and PEMF recharge a person's nervous system which is in effect one big electrical circuit.

When Matthew started coming back to us we realized that many of the things he learned before re-established themselves again quickly. They never really left him. He just couldn't express them the way he used to. It has been discovered that this is similar to many kids that have been recovered.

With the programs in the state we currently live in, Matthew has progressed as far as he can in biomedicine. As of mid 2009 we have decided to sell our home and move several states north to a more forward-thinking state that allows ABA, RDI occupational and speech therapy to help recover these kids. These are the next logical steps in his journey toward full recovery and I will not hinder his progress to achieve what he is capable of achieving.

If this journey has taught me anything, it has shown me this, we must never give up. Victory comes to those who never knew failure was an option. When people found out the Wright brothers were making a flying machine they told them it was impossible. They were ridiculed and humiliated by the naysayers.

Whenever someone tells me autism recovery is impossible, I look at my son. He has taught me more about life and love than I could have ever thought possible. Matthew's mother and I will be by his side, holding his hands as he continues to run into his future, and we will see him fly.

Appendix A – Treatable HBOT Conditions

Conditions for which Hyperbaric Oxygen Therapy has already been FDA approved as of 2008.

Actinomycosis: An infection caused by the Actinomyces israelii anaerobic bacteria, characterized by large growths on the head and neck of those affected.

Carbon Monoxide Poisoning: The inhalation of Carbon Monoxide, a colorless, odorless and tasteless gas leading to headaches, vertigo, flu-like symptoms and in large exposure cases, death.

Smoke Inhalation: The inhalation of smoke usually due to the victim being in close proximity to an uncontained fire without adequate ventilation. Can produce coughing, hoarseness, headache and eventually even death.

Clostridial Myonecrosis: Also called Gas Gangrene, it is an infection caused by the Clostridium anaerobic bacteria, characterized by swelling in the tissue surrounding the infection, sudden onset of pain, fever and confusion.

Cyanide Poisoning: Rare but potentially lethal poison mainly contracted from smoke inhalation of burning rubber, plastic etc., handling of photography chemicals, some types of rare plants and certain chemicals that the body converts into cyanide after ingestion.

Crush Injury: When a portion of the body is subjected to a large amount of pressure as can occur during a car crash.

Decompression Sickness: Also called 'the bends', it occurs when dissolved gases in the body form dangerous bubbles due to a sudden decrease in surrounding pressure.

Out of the Darkness

Diabetic Wounds: Wounds created due to poor circulation brought on by diabetes.

Necrotizing Soft Tissue Infections: Any of a host of bacterial infections with the potential to destroy muscle, skin or tissue.

Osteomyelitis: An infection occurring in bone or bone marrow.

Osteoradionecrosis: Tissue damage whose principle source is radiation whether from treatments for another condition or something else.

Severe Anemia: Extreme depletion of healthy, oxygenated red blood cells leading to fatigue.

Skin Grafts: The transplantation of skin in the treatment of severe injury due to trauma, burns or other skin conditions.

Thermal Burns: Injury resulting from excessive heat. Sources range from sunburn to fire.

Conditions for which Hyperbaric Oxygen Therapy has been used to help alleviate symptoms.

Autism and related disorders: A disorder affecting the brain characterized by any of a host of symptoms including but not limited to stemming, hyper-activity and impaired social skills.

AIDS / HIV: Acquired Immune Deficiency Syndrome, a weakening of the immune system caused by the Human Immunodeficiency Virus (HIV).

Allergies / Asthma: A form of hypersensitivity to a particular environmental trigger causing symptoms such as fever, runny nose, asthma or anaphylactic reactions.

Amyotrophic Lateral Sclerosis (ALS): Also known as Lou Gehrig's disease, it is a neurodegenerative disease in which motor neurons are destroyed over time.

Alzheimer's : A disorder affecting the brain characterized by dementia and in advanced stages violent acting out.

Arthritis – Rheumatoid, Osteoarthritis: The degenerative inflammation of joints in the body.

Atherosclerosis: An inflammation of the arterial blood vessels in the body.

Attention Deficit Disorder: Also known as ADD, it is an inability to focus on a single task for an extended period of time.

Bells Palsy: A neuropathy condition in which facial muscles are paralyzed.

Brain Injury / Encephalopathy: Damage to the brain of some kind.

Burns: Damage to the tissues of the body, usually epidermal, caused by heat, cold, electricity, chemicals, radiation or other factors.

Cerebral Palsy: A condition characterized by damage to the motor control centers of the brain causing impaired function.

Cancer: The progressive multiplication instead of elimination of damaged cells in the body.

Chronic Fatigue Immune Dysfunction: Condition in which fatigue, difficulty concentrating and muscle pain are all possible symptoms.

Coma: A state of unconsciousness which a patient can not recover from voluntarily.

Cosmetic Surgery: The use of medical procedures for non-life threatening conditions but focus on enhancing a patient's appearance in some way.

Crohn's Disease: A digestive disorder characterized by abdominal pain, diarrhea, vomiting or weight loss.

Dementia: A decline in mental function either from damage, disease or age. Can progress over time.

Out of the Darkness

Depression: A mental disorder characterized by feelings of hopelessness or low self-worth.

Diabetes: A condition in which a patient's metabolism doesn't operate properly causing hyperglycemia (high blood sugar levels).

Epilepsy / Seizures: A disorder in which the patient experiences either a loss of motor function or an excessive burst of it causing shaking or seizing.

Fibromyalgia: A disorder characterized by chronic widespread pain and sensitivity that can come on suddenly.

Hearing Loss: A decline in the ear's ability to pick up vibrations in the air and translate them into meaningful data for the brain. Can be caused for a number of different reasons / diseases.

Heart Disease: Any of a host of diseases affecting the heart and impeding function.

Hepatitis: An injury to the liver due to the presence of inflammatory cells.

Infection: The introduction of a foreign organism resistant to the body's natural defense mechanisms.

Injury Healing: The natural process of healing done by the body.

Interstitial Cystitis: A disease of the urinary bladder characterized by increased urination frequency or urgency and or pain.

Lupus: A disease of the autoimmune system where the body's immune system attacks its own cells and tissues.

Lyme Disease: An infectious tick-borne disease characterized with fever, headaches, joint and muscle pain.

Macular Degeneration: A disorder characterized by a loss of vision in the center of a person's visual field.

Memory Loss: A brain disorder in which a patient loses portions of their memory. Can be due to a host of different diseases including Alzheimer's and Parkinson's.

Menopause Symptoms: Occurs when a woman's body reaches the end of its menstruation period. Symptoms include irregular periods, mood swings, loss of sleep and hot flashes.

Migraines: Severe, in most cases, headaches resulting in diminished function.

Multiple Chemical Sensitivity: A sensitivity to exposure of low dose chemicals freely found in today's environments such as smoke, plastics and paints.

Multiple Sclerosis: An autoimmune disorder where a person's own immune system attacks their central nervous system.

Near Drowning: The involuntary flooding of the lungs, usually with water, that inhibits the body's ability to respire.

Neuropathy: Impaired function of motor, sensory and autonomic neurons.

Ocular Conditions: Conditions affecting the eye.

Orthopedic: Related to the musculoskeletal system.

Osteoporosis: A bone disease characterized by a decrease in bone mineral density. Can lead to bone fracture.

Parkinson's: A condition affecting the central nervous system that affects motor skills among other things.

Post-Polio: A viral disease that can be spread infectiously. Can lead to a host of issues including paralysis and death.

Post-Surgery: The recovery period after a person has undergone surgery.

Reflex Sympathetic Dystrophy: A condition that can have any or all of the following symptoms, burning pain, bone and skin alteration, profuse sweating, swelled tissues or touch sensitivity.

Rheumatoid Arthritis: Inflammation of the joints due to the autoimmune system attacking them.

Rheumatic Diseases: Blanket term for any disease affecting the bones, heart, joints, kidneys, lungs, or skin.

Seizures: An involuntary convulsion of the body's motor functions. Can range in severity.

Spinal Cord Injury: Any injury to the spine.

Sports Injury: Any injury caused during high stress sport activity.

Stroke: A major loss of oxygen to a portion of the brain causing a loss of function in the affected area. Can lead to death.

Surgery: Any type of medical procedure in which medical tools or techniques are used on a patient.

Traumatic Brain Injury: Any injury to the brain leading to high stress of any portion of it. Can be caused by any number of conditions or incidents.

General Wound Healing: The body's natural ability to heal itself.

Appendix B - Interviews

Dan Rossignol M.D. _____

Attended:	University of Virginia Undergraduate School
Graduated:	Medical College of Virginia
Residency:	University of Virginia. Clinical Assistant Professor, University of Virginia
Status:	Family practice established 2006, Melbourne Florida
Projects:	Hyperbaric Oxygen Therapy

Interviewer – You have two sons who both have autism. Is that how you got involved in hyperbarics as a possible treatment?

Dr. Rossignol – That's right. That's the only reason I got involved in hyperbarics. Before that I was a family practitioner. My wife had discovered it from other moms with autistic children. I was very skeptical at first. I thought it would be a waste of money but got a chamber to try it out after realizing that the form of therapy we were going to attempt involved no harm to our children in doing so.

Hard chamber therapy can be dangerous if not closely monitored. What we were going to use was soft therapy with a home chamber. These chambers are so low in pressure that you really don't have to worry about things such as barotraumas – pressure and pain in places like the ear. The max pressure is equivalent to being about nine feet underwater. It's like diving to the bottom of a home pool.

One night I was sitting in the living room and my oldest son, who up to then had only spoken one to two words at a time, walked up to me and said, 'Open the gate, please.'. I nearly fell over. He was referring to the small gate we had placed across the stairs to keep our kids from falling down them.

When my younger son started hyperbarics he was saying one word at a time. By his twentieth treatment he was putting several words together as well.

My eyes were opened suddenly and I knew something was going on but just not sure what it was. I started researching literature for hyperbarics and autism but couldn't find any studies but one. I realized that I needed to start documenting and get involved in studies to figure out what it was doing and how it was doing it.

Interviewer – Have you seen much resistance to its use in the medical community?

Dr. Rossignol – I discovered that most physicians that use it don't know why it works. Most don't have the time to research or perform studies. I spend a lot of time wondering how it works. It's one of those things that can be proven to work but can't be fully explained yet so it isn't accepted.

Even if you do a study no one really pays attention until someone else comes along and does the same one again to reconfirm your findings. Because of this it can take quite some time before things become accepted as mainstream. There's been a few times where I had parent's pediatrician yelling at me on the phone for treating their kids with it. Most are not confrontational and many understand once I explain to them that the methods used are safe and what we are trying to do actually has some research behind it.

I speak at a lot of conferences and work on papers and research to help change the preconceived opinions out there and educate others as best as possible. I am always bouncing ideas around and reading new articles on the subject.

Interviewer – Can you briefly explain the therapy?

Dr. Rossignol – Hyperbaric therapy is well established in the medical community for wound treatments and the like. It hasn't been widely accepted for autism and neurological disorders yet. I've found that usually for neurological conditions, most people use forty dives –or treatments, sometimes eighty. Roughly 95% of children that show improvement do so within the forty dive range. About five percent of kids improve around sixty to sixty-five dives. Some kids do not improve at all with hyperbarics so it's not a cure-all by any means.

Although highly unlikely, there are some instances where children improved after two or three dives. The recommendation is forty. The initial dive schedule is not staggered so that the child can receive the full benefits of the treatment at once.

Hyperbaric therapy doesn't allow red blood cells to carry more oxygen, they are already 97% O2 saturated. It simply forces more O_2 into the body's plasma, the clear fluid that red blood cells travel through. This allows the oxygen to travel places in the body that red blood cells can't even reach.

It decreases inflammation. Inflammation of the brain is a major indicator of autism so it might not even be the increase in oxygen but the decrease in inflammation that is helping.

It supplies more oxygen to the brain and improves mitochondrial function at the cellular level. It kills anaerobic bacteria in the gut and other oxygen poor places.

It increases the production of adult stem cells. Stem cells may help in the longer term.

One problem with studies is that there are two components to hyperbaric therapy. There's pressure and oxygen. Since both are being utilized at once, it's harder to tell which is doing what to help. It appears that pressure is what helps lower inflammation. You can get the same increase in oxygen content from a hyperbaric session as you can by just breathing from an oxygen mask. This tells us that pressure is a big factor as well.

Oxygen increases inflammation while pressure decreases it. In autism we are tackling inflammation in the brain. Hyperbarics helps proportionally those autistic children with severe levels of inflammation. We think that low pressure works because even at 1.3 atmospheres, you're 30% above sea level so you get a 30% increase in oxygen intake automatically, just from the pressure. Since you don't have something like a diabetic wound that would impede flow, you can get by with a lot less pressure.

Interviewer – Do you use chelation as well?

Dr. Rossignol – If I do decide that chelation might help one of my patients, we do thorough testing first to see if there is an increased amount of heavy metals in their system. We won't suggest it otherwise since it would be useless. We also try other options such as vitamins before moving to chelation if things do not improve. I like to see if the simple, less-intrusive methods are effective before having to move on to things that could potentially pose higher risks, are harder to do or are more expensive.

Interviewer – Have you seen a surge in interest in the therapy?

Dr. Rossignol – There has been a huge increase in the number of people inquiring about hyperbarics in just the last few years. It used to be only extreme cases that were coming in, but now parents who feel their children are even slightly delayed are bringing them in to give them the best possible start and try and prevent problems.

There is so much more awareness now in some communities and parents are being really proactive. It's not uncommon to see people with children who display very mild autism to come in for treatments whereas three or four years ago they would have just waited, feeling their child was just delayed.

Twenty years ago if your doctor said do x, y and z that's what you did. Today people ask are you sure? I want another opinion. They do things like research on the internet.

Interviewer – Any notable recovery cases?

Dr. Rossignol – We don't use hyperbarics solely for autism related cases. It's been used for stroke recovery, cerebral palsy, near drowning and other neurological disorders as well.

A few years ago a lady came in who had had a stroke two years prior. She was losing her vision. After treatments, she got her vision back. It fades again every six months and she comes back in for 10 to 20 treatments to get it back. She, like some, do it for maintenance.

A twelve year old boy would repeatedly bang his head against the wall and bite his skin to the point that he had blood dripping off his hands from chewing them. He had only ever been treated with standard pharmaceutical drugs. We put him on a few vitamin supplements and he's a lot calmer now.

A guy had a stroke and became wheelchair bound some years ago. With hyperbarics and physical therapy, he was able to walk again.

Kids too numerous to count, have improved. One child had diarrhea every day from birth. After three sessions of HBOT his stools were completely normal. Some weeks later he said his first word. At the end of forty dives he was putting words together. Many kids are able to get off medication after HBOT. It has helped with attention, receptive understanding, eye contact, speaking, hyperactivity, sleeping through the night, bedwetting and biting.

Interviewer – Is there anything else you'd like to add?

Dr. Rossignol – I've seen a majority of kids get better with HBOT. If my own kids didn't have autism, I probably wouldn't be as driven as I am for a cure. I find it so rewarding when parents see their children get better. Parents with autistic children seem driven to find a cure because they had seen their child before autism. They had seen them developing normally and reach a level, then regress. It's like they had their children stolen from them right before their eyes. A lot of doctors that get into Defeat Autism Now are directly influenced by autism. Either their own children have it or a niece or nephew and so on. If it affects you or your family, it's personal and you do something about it. If not, then you tend to think it's bad but usually don't really get involved.

Out of the Darkness

Mary Megson M.D. _____

Graduated:	University of Virginia
Residency:	Boston Floating Hospital, Tufts
Status:	Director of Developmental Pediatrics, Children's Hospital in Richmond. Pediatric practice
Projects:	Autism recovery therapies

Interviewer – Can you tell me how you became involved in autism research and recovery?

Dr. Megson – When I first started working with early child development, I noticed more and more kids coming in that had reached their language and developmental milestones after their one year old birthdays only to lose them before their second birthdays. I felt that I needed to find out what was going on.

I discovered a doctor in California doing parallel studies with vitamins and discovered vitamin A was lacking from these children's diets. Vitamin A is naturally an oil at room temperature. We have turned it into a solid in our food processing procedures. Cod Liver Oil contains naturally occurring vitamin A. This is what we started these children on. Many started coming back.

Receptors that allow cells to communicate to each other break down without vitamin A. This is why, once this is repaired, there can be dramatically improved results. These children's cells aren't being destroyed, they just can't communicate to each other.

There are genetic indicators for autism but that's not the entire picture. There are environmental triggers as well. Just look at a map of a state like Texas, detailing autism cases. Overlay that same map with power plant and factory emission's pollution and the numbers match.

Many of these children have histories of neurological disorder in their families as well.

This is only one piece of the very large puzzle. Others are uncovering more every day.

Interviewer – Do these children suddenly lose their abilities?

Dr. Megson – Autism is a gradual decline of function and ability. It does not occur suddenly all at once so it's difficult to find a single factor for its cause. Have you ever had the feeling that the room was spinning and you were going to faint? You're there but not really. This is what autism is sort of like except the feeling lasts a lot longer than a few seconds.

Things such as heavy metals in vaccines, among other things, can push susceptible children's systems over the tipping point. These kids are hit with the MMR among other things all at the same time. That's four different live viruses attacking their system simultaneously. We normally only fight off one virus at a time usually. We catch something and our body attacks it, displaying fever, handles it. We don't usually have to fight off four at once.

I'm not against vaccines. I'm a strong advocate for them. I don't want to go back to a pre-polio world when children can be protected from harmful diseases now. We can all agree that if there was a test we could give before vaccinating them that would allow us to detect if a child was potentially susceptible to autism, we would give it. Everyone's body chemistry is unique and that needs to be taken into consideration.

Vaccine multi-dose vials include metals, previously therimosol now aluminum, as a means to kill any bacteria that could potentially transfer from one patient to the next if the vaccine became contaminated. This type of danger is non-existent with single-dose vials. Single-dose vials are more expensive to manufacture however, so the distribution standard is multi-dose.

Interviewer – Have you noticed any kind of shift in the medical community regarding autism diagnosis and treatment?

Dr. Megson – When I began researching autism, there were not too many in the medical community that understood it. I only had three gastrointestinal physicians I could refer patients too. More and more people are under standing things and getting involved because it has become an epidemic. So many are affected either directly or indirectly now.

Interviewer – There are some that feel recovery is not possible. What are your thoughts on that?

Dr. Megson – Recovery is possible and has occurred. What you have to remember is that those that are susceptible always have the possibility of falling back into autism due to any of the triggers that contribute to it. I had an 18 year old that had displayed no signs of autism. She had to have a shot before entering college and then became autistic.

Interviewer – When did you discover gluten-casein as a possible issue?

Dr. Megson – Gluten-casein was brought to my attention by a mother of an autistic child that had already discovered a link. I noticed that many of my patients had diets full of pizza, cookies ice cream and so on. Their digestive systems can't break down the last part of gluten or casein before it enters the bloodstream.

This causes opiates in the blood. In some cases these children hallucinate as if on some sort of high. I had one girl seeing rats running around in her peripheral vision. These kids are addicts to gluten-casein, raiding the fridge in the middle of the night. They have to be weaned off products containing these proteins gradually.

Interviewer – What are your thoughts regarding chelation therapy?

Dr. Megson – Chelation has gotten a bad rap. It is not the dangerous, highly questionable therapy of times past. When most think of it, they think of large doses of lead that have to be drastically expelled. These children have minute doses of heavy metals in their systems that need removal because their genetic make-up leaves them more vulnerable than the rest of us.

Heavy metals can't be directly measured since once exposure occurs the body's tissues absorb them almost immediately. The test that used to be done to detect them was the hair test. Hair was examined since some metals are captured in it in a state that is easily recovered. That has been replaced in recent years by a much more accurate test in which a person's PH is examined.

Interviewer – Are there any other types of therapy's you use for autism recovery?

Dr. Megson – Hyperbaric oxygen therapy. When you say that, many people think of divers and the bends in giant metal rooms. There are other types of chamber therapy now. Soft chamber therapy is relatively harmless to the patient but the benefits can sometimes be astounding.

Interviewer – Thank you so much for your time. Is there anything you want to leave us with?

Dr. Megson – Just to get the word out as much as possible that recovery is possible.

Out of the Darkness

J.B. Handley_____

Co-Founder: Generation Rescue – parent driven organization dedicated to eradicating autism and educating care-givers of possible recovery methods

---

Interviewer – Can you tell me what event or events led you to become an advocate for autism awareness?

Mr. Handley – My son, who is now six years old. His diagnosis is what led me to advocacy. It became readily apparent to me that something had happened to him rather than this being something he was born with. The more I learned, the more my outrage grew and the more committed I became to trying to spread what I viewed to other families.

My son's decent into autism was a textbook case of a normal child receiving too many vaccines, becoming overloaded, losing his bearings and ultimately being diagnosed with autism.

He has since experienced a significant recovery although it remains ongoing. He's now attending neuro-typical kindergarten which is a highlight of our life. We're gratified with his improvement to date and we continue to treat him bio-medically. Our goal is to get him back one hundred percent to the child he was supposed to be.

Interviewer – How did your relationship with the Faiella family form?

Mr. Handley – Daniel emailed our organization trying to get the word out because he wanted us to know that something was working for his son. Parents are really the source for every major breakthrough in autism treatment. That's because they're the first to try it and the first to see the results. Daniel epitomizes a parent who wants to take the pain that he and his own family have been through and try and use that to help other families.

By the time he reached me he was talking about both hyperbarics and stem cell therapy.

Interviewer – Can you discuss Generation Rescue? How it came about and if it's accomplished what you expected?

Mr. Handley – Generation Rescue was founded in 2005 by myself and my wife out of a desire to try and give back in some ways to the community of parents that were teaching us how to recover our own son.

One element that we felt was missing was a single website, a single source for everything related to how to treat your child. We knew what it felt like to be a parent with a newly diagnosed child. The only thing that you want to know is what do I do now. That is a very elusive answer and we tried to make it more clear.

Information was disparate and hard for the average person to appreciate the level of trauma that a parent of a newly diagnosed child is going through. The amount of research required to become proficient was tens if not hundreds of hours. My wife and I felt that if we put this all in one place we could save parents time that could be better used in other ways and give them a real roadmap, a real game plan to try and recover their child.

Interviewer – Has Generation Rescue reached a level you wished it too? Has it fallen short of your expectations?

Mr. Handley – You know, it's a double-edged sword. I wish it wasn't as popular a site as it is because that means we've still got our work cut out for us and we want to see the rate of autism decrease dramatically. That hasn't happened yet so on one level I don't think we've fulfilled our mission yet.

It's certainly far bigger, has far more volunteers, far more web traffic and is far more well known than my wife and I ever imagined it would be. In no small part to Jenny McCarthy.

Interviewer – How did she get involved?

Mr. Handley – Jenny's story is the ideal story for why we created Generation Rescue. Her son was diagnosed, she found the website on her own like any other parent and she initiated treatment for her son using some of the guidelines of the website and she immediately started to see improvement.

Because of her sense that we had been the catalyst for her to open her mind that autism was something you could recover from she's paid us back a thousand-fold by becoming part of our organization.

Interviewer – Can you explain the 'green our vaccines' movement?

Mr. Handley – Green our vaccines is Jenny McCarthy's idea. She deserves one hundred percent of the credit for the slogan, the movement, the rally and everything else. We were nothing but a supporter of Jenny's initiative.

Jenny's purpose in doing that is to point out how toxic vaccines really are today and challenge parents and health authorities to think about what's being injected into the precious bodies of our babies.

Interviewer – What is the Rescue Angel network?

Mr. Handley – Rescue Angels are parent volunteers all over the world organized on our website by geography. Their sole purpose is to help other parents get started on the path to recovery for their children. There are more than a thousand of them now and they're the backbone of who we are. They represent a microcosm of the biomedical community of parents. They're there to help others.

Our estimate is that they've helped well over twenty-five thousand families get started with treatment for their kids. They are there for advice and support. The two things parents of newly diagnosed kids really need but do not get from the mainstream.

Interviewer – Are there any forms of treatment you advocate? Any you oppose?

Mr. Handley – We try to be as inclusive as possible at Generation Rescue for anything that might help kids. We view the only credible source for that information to be other parents. Until we're recovering one hundred percent of the kids, we haven't figured it all out yet. I think the other thing is that we remain both very open and very humble about what's best for any one child.

Unfortunately, we can't instantly tell a parent, these are the forms of intervention that are going to work best for your kid specifically. We just don't know how to do that. So what we try to do is keep parents informed as to what other parents say is working best.

I would never use the word never when it comes to biomedical intervention and our role is not to define and categorize what works and what doesn't but rather to assemble the information the parents are generating every day.

Interviewer – Are there any other projects or ideas you want to get across with your organization?

Mr. Handley – There are two important things we're trying to do simultaneously. One is to make sure as many parents of children with autism are informed that there are options for recovery and that recovery is real. The second primary mission is to inform all parents that they can amend their kids' vaccination schedule. Because we genuinely believe that if most parents took a more prudent approach to vaccination we would watch the rates of autism plummet severely. This includes reducing the total number of vaccines their children receive, doing them later, staggering them. Not giving six on one day, not giving them while a child is on antibiotics, not giving them while a child's sick. Precautionary principle throughout the entire process of any vaccines they might consider getting, not going with the recommended schedule. The schedule recommended by the vaccine manufacturers.

Interviewer – Any opinions regarding stem cell therapy?

Mr. Handley – I've read a lot about it and talked to other parents that have done it. It makes a ton of sense in why it's working for these kids. The rate of positive feedback on the children that have done it appears to be very high compared to other interventions I've seen. I'm extremely hopeful that there can be a cheaper domestic source so that more children can be helped.

I think Daniel singularly deserves a ton of credit for raising the awareness level on what stem cells have done for his son.

Interviewer – Have you noticed a lot of resentment from certain groups within the mainstream community?

Mr. Handley – It's been extreme and it's safe to say that all of the parents that speak loudly have a target on their backs because they are not only challenging orthodoxy, they are challenging reputations and profit. The truth always bears out in the end but in the meantime there's going to be resistance. Mark my words, it will get uglier before it gets fixed.

So, yes, I would say that the level of opposition, criticism that we have personally received as an organization, as individuals has been extremely high and will likely continue to be so.

I think if you're a student of history, that any new truth, any inconvenient truth, goes through this process and we just happen to be right in the middle of it.

Interviewer – Do you see any similarities between this issue and the big tobacco debate of the nineties?

Mr. Handley – It's wildly similar to tobacco. The analogies are almost endless. I really am a student of the tobacco lung cancer conflict because I do think it's the closest analogy we have and it's one that most people are grounded in to be able to understand the commonality.

But one of the most interesting things is to see the "scientists" of the tobacco companies fill our airwaves in interview after interview making all the same arguments. It's the level of the toxins and in cigarettes it's far lower and so forth. It's the same bag of tricks. It's the same studies using the same smoke and mirrors. We've seen this movie before. We've seen all the tobacco company executives with their hands up in front of congress, all saying that cigarettes do not cause lung cancer. Yet we sit here and wonder how a cover-up of something of this magnitude is possible and yet there it was not fifteen, twenty years ago.

The difference is at least the target of tobacco companies were adults with knowledge. There aren't many of us who feel particularly empathetic for an eighty-five year old smoker who dies of lung cancer because we say, they had full information. These are kids and parents who are trusting doctors who are being misled. That, I think, is far more tragic.

I would far rather my kid become a smoker than have autism.

Interviewer – Is there anything you'd like to add?

Mr. Handley – I'd just like to say I think Daniel is a real hero. It's one thing to hop on a plane, go to Costa Rica and have your son treated with stem cells. It's another to bring the media along with you. He does that to try and help other people. I'm grateful and wish there were more people that had his integrity to speak the truth. He has viewed his son's recovery, I think appropriately, as an unbelievable gift for which he has a burden to give back. He appears to be doing that in spades.

Out of the Darkness

Mark Squibb _____

Chairman/ Founder: Whole Health Network – Pulsed Electromagnetic
Field Therapy (PEMF)
Research and Technology

www.wholehealthnetwork.com

_____

Interviewer – Can you tell us a little about PEMF and how you became involved with it?

Mr. Squibb – PEMF is an interesting technology. It's really old and nothing short of amazing. As for getting involved, it's a long story but basically my mom got sick and was diagnosed with lung cancer. I started frantically searching for technologies that could be of assistance to her and bought an early version of a PEMF machine combining its use with some other things.

Within about four months, her small cell lung cancer attenuated to the extent that it pretty much went away. This was a very aggressive form of cancer and what was amazing was that she was near death when we started and just really backed out of a whole bunch of really ugly symptoms. She went from a very high level of what you call tumor markers to semi-normal.

In the end I had this device that I didn't know much about. All I knew was I had seen my mother get markedly better with it. I needed to understand more so I wrapped my head around this technology to see what I could learn. As time progressed, I began to branch into ortho-chemical and ortho-energenic views.

Since then, I've learned a lot about many different categories of technology and am now focusing on more integrated goals, nutritional, electrophysiology, energetic-physiology, that sort of thing. I'm a technology integrator by breeding and have spent many years in the software industry dealing with particularly complex systems. I've found that physiology as a principle from an engineering standpoint isn't a whole lot different from working with complicated software systems.

Interviewer – What drew you to consider PEMF as a form of autism treatment?

Mr. Squibb – I was in Florida a couple of weeks ago and met Daniel Faiella through a fellow colleague. One of the things I'm constantly doing is traveling various places, conferences etc. asking questions. I am always asking why to everything. One thing that began popping up again and again was neuro-physiology and neurologically degenerate situations.

We have a research clinic where we use a combination of pulse magnetic field generators as well as various detoxification methods. We've seen some amazing turnaround in very severe pathologies, particularly of the neurological type. Like parkinsons, stroke and Lou Gerigs for example.

We've had cases of parkinsons where individuals came in presenting either neurological dysfunction or tremor symptoms or both. In each case we witnessed 50 to 75% attenuation in neurological dysfunction within the first 30 minutes.

One lady with parkinsons that we were working with for 6 months was recently told by her doctors that they must have made a mistake on her initial diagnosis. She no longer fits the parkinsons definition.

After looking at our findings and applying them to autism, I discovered that there appears to exist a hybrid dysfunction consisting of a combination of toxins produced by pathogenic organisms as well as an addiction phenomenon going on where these little organisms make neurological drugs that the person ends up becoming addicted to. This creates a whole range of dysfunctions.

So, what I started seeing was a set of pretty common factors across all these neurological things. Then I made the trip to Florida and met Daniel after talking to him on the phone. When I saw Matthew and listened intently to his parents tell me his story, I began to notice the same neurological commonality to what I had had success with in the past.

A few months ago I met a doctor at a conference who mentioned why vaccines may play a part as a frequent trigger of autism. His outlook, the hidden challenge in vaccines isn't mercury, it's actually the fact that they all are heavy containers of aluminum, particularly ionic aluminum. What's special about aluminum is that it is a flocculating or coagulating agent. It's actually used in city water treatment plants to treat muddy water. The aluminum ions in the water clump together with the mud settling out. If you take this sort of clumping agent and put it in the body it becomes a clotting agent.

The fancy word is zeta potential. It is the energetic property of fluid that enables things to remain suspended. So in blood, for example, as long as the erythrocytes etc. in it remain suspended and separated, everything flows. If you, by accident or injection, present more clotting agent than the body can tolerate you will selectively plug the microvasculature.

What this doctor observed while working with autistic kids was that the majority of them presented with autism within hours of vaccination by displaying neurological symptoms identical to stroke. If you look at autistic children you usually notice their facial symmetry. An eye may drift inward, outward or down. The lip may drift downward. That sort of thing. When we see this in the elderly we immediately send them to the hospital because we know they are having a stroke. When it happens to a child we say oh, gee…that's interesting.

We don't even notice and what's happening is this clotting, not only driven by aluminum but also by the body's inflammatory response to it, is causing a perfect storm condition within the child's body. A sort of damage roulette happens. Blood flow, not just to the brain, but throughout the entire body is shut down. Places like the gut, the bone marrow, anywhere that's supported by small vessels has the potential to become clogged. When this occurs, any tissue downstream of the blood supply chokes and the child's body shuts down there. Symptoms seem random but they are actually localized to the area(s) that unfortunately got blocked.

If a child goes back for a successive vaccination before they've had a chance to recover from the first hit to their system, then the damage becomes cumulative. You get a trauma that is often the catalyst putting the child into an unrecoverable state.

Sometimes these disorders present as ADHD, sometimes you don't see any neurological symptoms at all, Sometimes its immunological or digestive. There always appears to be some type of damage preventing these children from recovering and thriving. If you take someone that's healthy and inoculate them they may not even notice but inoculate someone that's starving or been subjected to cold or flu and is already immunologically loaded there is the potential to weaken them further.

Vaccinations are by no means the whole problem. The real problem is the fact that the kids aren't healthy enough to tolerate the hit they get from them. The children end up in a deadlock situation. There are different categories of concurrent damage that are permanently preventing proper healing from occurring.

Interviewer – Can you discuss more about aluminum?

Mr. Squibb – There are natural paths that carry aluminum out of the body. If a child has a dysfunctional methalation or detoxification path, they are more susceptible to accumulation. They receive a blast of aluminum which over time is filtered out of their system. Aluminum accumulation isn't the real issue either. The real issue is that aluminum causes the clots, aluminum becomes secondary. The clots themselves prevent the circulation. The clots are what cause permanent damage. In most cases the aluminum goes away but the problems caused by them remains.

I call this scenario the autistic cascade and it is composed of at least three stages. The first is the child ends up in a weakened state due to some combination of environmental, food toxins, glucose process, you name it. Second, the child is hit with vaccine while their systems are already down. Third, the clumping creates blockages shutting down the vasculature causing the immune system to fail. This allows the bugs to move in.

These kids have so many harmful pathogens in their systems that their immune system goes into deadlock. Going on an anti-biotic to handle one type of pathogen allows other harmful ones more room to move in and grow. You suppress one and another blooms in its place. This is why conventional anti-pathogen intervention doesn't work well in these cases.

Out of the Darkness

All you end up doing is moving stuff around and generally making things worse. These bad pathogens mature in the child's system and begin producing their own toxins further suppressing the child's healing abilities and keeping the cycle going.

So not only do you have the brain damage that comes from the original stroke but you also end up with another category of brain damage from the sludge all these pathogens are producing. The body pools its resources in an attempt to generate anti-toxins but in doing so it steals from the digestive system thereby creating problems there as well.

Interviewer – Have you used PEMF technology on autistic kids?

Mr. Squibb – We are working on setting that up currently. The initial steps are to build a protocol to optimize autism recovery that can be practically applied. The goal is not to say hey, let's throw everything at the problem but to go through and build a model which suggests prioritization and flow in a decision process. I'm talking like an engineer now. List the first priority, the second and so forth as opposed to hitting these poor kids with everything at once. The point is that we need to sequence things and use all the things that work to their highest potential.

There are many recovery tools out there such as hyperbarics, pulse magnetism, ionic baths, detoxification, gut reparation, probiotics, stem cells etc. Each one of these interventions has a collection of assumptions about what works verses what doesn't. Utilizing each method and understanding the assumptions regarding each one that have to be met prior to it working really helps in understanding. All this stuff is sequencing the best order of treatment.

We've set up an assessment portal site as a place for doctors, care providers and the like to all share ideas and results in order to build an integrated protocol with a program called care fusion. It is designed as a way to coordinate and build custom interventions on a per case basis.

Another effective tool is the pulse magnetic field generator. Treatment can be localized to a particular region and they are dramatically effective at restoring normal cell physiology. You can work on the digestive tract then work toward the liver and gall bladder etc.

The body is made up of compartments that are broken down into smaller compartments all the way down to inside the individual cells. Pulse generators activate detoxification so it's important to understand what needs to be detoxified in what order. Attempting to detoxify one compartment without clearing another first is likely to cause a concentration of toxins in a specific area which can be even more hazardous.

Out of the Darkness

Donna Gates_____

Status: Nutritional Therapist, Lecturer and Author of 'The Body
             Ecology Diet'
Projects: Autism awareness, prevention and recovery

Interviewer – Miss Gates, can you tell me your views on whether or not the source of autism and autism related symptoms is nutritional in nature.

Miss Gates – Not really just nutritional. In short, our theory on the cause is this. There is a series of events that occur. Remember, this generation of women who are now having children were raised on lots of antibiotics. They have system yeast infections in their bloodstreams. The medical profession does not want this to be know as a cause of autism because it opens up a huge can of worms...not just vaccines...but also the fact that we went crazy with antibiotics...prescribed them for everything...and it is affecting our next generation of babies. Making them susceptible to becoming autistic.

Then there is the fact that today's babies are not as healthy as previous generations. They never get strong immune systems in place before they are vaccinated...especially since they are vaccinated so early in life...like day of birth or within the first few weeks.

Some draw that unlucky straw and instead of being healthy enough on the day of vaccination to fight against the pathogen that is injected into them...they succumb to the virus and it infects the whole body and the brain. The brain becomes inflamed and some cells are damaged...especially in the Broca region (left side) dealing with communication. This needs to be repaired which is how a colleague of mine became involved with stem cells at ICM.

Interviewer – If the intestinal ecosystems of these children can be returned to their proper state, then their autism symptoms should decrease. Have you witnessed or know of studies where this has been the case?

Miss Gates – There are no good studies done to date...but the doctors working with autistic children have come to realize the gut is huge. You must heal the gut. It is a well accepted fact now. We see it working. It makes sense because the children have nutritional deficiencies, you must correct the health of the gut to correct nutritional deficiencies. Also there is a direct connection between the gut and the brain. The gut is our second brain...or enteric nervous system.

Interviewer – Any views regarding Hyperbaric Oxygen therapy and how it might affect the gut flora?

Miss Gates – The benefit of HBOT is to the brain mostly. It can help bring oxygen to those cells damaged by the infection in the brain due to the vaccine. Here's a new thought...it can also strengthen the immune system. I think if a child got into an oxygen chamber when the brain infection was occurring...they would most likely not become autistic. Oxygen has been shown to be very effective against viruses.

If they have strong immune systems due to the gut flora (75-89% of the immune system is in the gut associated lymphoid tissue) they would also be far better able to then fight infection by the virus in the vaccine. We are trying to correct and heal a child from autism...and sadly we need to be standing by ready to prevent autism with tools like this.

Interviewer – Any views on adult stem cell treatment?

Miss Gates – It is expensive and for too many unobtainable at this time... and now they are diagnosing children much earlier. If the parent can put the child on a gluten free, sugar free, anti-candida, probiotic rich diet they can begin to pull the child out. Oxygen to repair the brain cell damage would be a wise idea. But for those many older children and adults I really do believe that adult stem cells will become one of the most important tools and a must.

The child needs to have a body and a brain in the best condition possible before he receives the stem cells to make them most effective. The child should be as physically healthy as possible and on a diet like ours for six months to a year so that their immune system is stronger and their yeast infection is under control. All these children have yeast infections. Anti-fungal drugs are not the answer.

Out of the Darkness

The child's digestive health must be good so they are not protein malnourished, deficient in fatty acids needed by the brain, and deficient in minerals. Their thyroid and adrenals need to test strong and in balance. This way the child has the energy to heal. They must have a healthy inner ecosystem in place, for many reasons. And then I'd like to see the child have a brain scan. We need information on the cells. We must make sure the brain is vibrating at the right frequency. Is there still a lot of inflammation in the brain and the stem cells have to first go to fight that before it can focus on regrowing new brain cells. As those brain cells begin to grow, the need to be trained with neuro-feedback techniques like those developed by Dr. Penny Montgomery and Margaret Ayers.

I would love to see research done on a group of children who got all of this. I think we'd be thrilled with the results. They still need help with learning skills that were not developed naturally when the child's brain and body were ill, like social skill training. Son Rise and RDI are great for this. Some may need speech classes. But we can heal these children. There is so much determination, passion, intelligent research and love in the parents of these children. The world needs to understand that there are millions of young men and women who are on the battle field every day in their homes fighting a painful battle to bring the truth to our attention. The truth is these children are showing us our future. And we need to act immediately to change the way we eat, the environment we live in and the way we practice medicine. Drugs have damaged us, environmental poisons and poisonous foods have been with us for four generations now. The kids are showing us the results of our greed and desire to have what we humans want, and not what nature decrees. Our arrogance has brought us here. It's time to be humble. Autism brings families to their knees. The rest of the world should be supporting them. They are showing us what we must do or we will all be on our knees in humble apology.

Interviewer – Is there a set protocol for 'flushing' the digestive system in order to bring it back into balance? This has to be done carefully to avoid the patient getting sick correct?

Miss Gates – Every child is a unique experiment of one. But the BEDROK program has been in place for over seven years now. The parents know what works and the wonderful information archived there is priceless. It is a great place to send families. Lots of attention and love.

Interviewer – Can you provide your viewpoint on what Matthew's parents are attempting to do for him?

Miss Gates – They are perfect examples of the intelligence and devotion these parents have. They don't realize it at first, but eventually do, that this challenge has called up an inner strength and greatness in them that would not have been there if their love for their child hadn't inspired it.

Daniel is amazing. He is so willing to share what he learns with others. I always tell him, he has such an important role in bringing out the truth.

The truth with be coming clear to us eventually but Daniel, and parents like him, are making it happen today not in a decade when it's too late.

Autism could be like cancer, a big business with no real solutions. Mystery about the cause but no final answers.

Daniel and other parents like him and certain courageous, committed doctors in Defeat Autism Now, are working together to make sure autism is a nightmare that has a happy ending.

Appendix C - Dr. Megson's Congressional Speech

Autism and Attention Deficit Disorder in Vaccinated Children
By: Megson, Mary Norfleet, MD
TESTIMONY PRESENTED TO GOVERNMENT REFORM COMMIT-
TEE HEARING ON AUTISM
Washington, DC, April 6, 2000

Mr. Chairman, Honorable Dan Burton and members of the committee; My name is Mary Norfleet Megson. I am a board-certified pediatrician, Fellowship trained in Child Development, a member of the American Academy of Pediatrics and Assistant Professor of Pediatrics at Medical College of Virginia. I have practiced pediatrics for twenty-two years, the last fifteen years seeing only children with Developmental Disabilities, which include learning disabilities, attention deficit hyperactivity disorder, cerebral palsy, mental retardation and autism.

In 1978, I learned as a resident at Boston Floating Hospital that the incidence of autism was one in 10,000 children. Over the last ten years I have watched the incidence of autism skyrocket to 1/300-1/600 children.[1] Over the last nine months, I have treated over 1,200 children in my office. Ninety percent of these children are autistic and from the Richmond area alone. The State Department of Education reports that there are only 1522 autistic students in the state of Virginia.

MHMR agencies have created local infant intervention programs, and have had a hard time keeping up with the numbers of delayed infants and toddlers. I have served as advisor to the City of Richmond and the surrounding counties as they have established entire programs for autistic children that fill multiple classes in several schools in each district. The segment of children with "regressive autism," the form where children develop normally for a period of time then lose skills and sink into autism most commonly at

151

Out of the Darkness

18-24 months of age, is increasing at a phenomenal rate. I am seeing multiple children in the same family affected, including in the last week four cases of "autistic regression" developing in four-year-old children after their MMR and DPT vaccination. In the past, this was unheard of.

In the vast majority of these cases, one parent reports night blindness[2] or other rarer disorders which are caused by a genetic defect in a G protein,[3] where they join cell membrane receptors, which are activated by retinoids, neurotransmitters, hormones, secretin and other protein messengers. G proteins are cellular proteins that upgrade or downgrade signals in sensory organs that regulate touch, taste, smell, hearing and vision. They are found all over the body, in high concentration in the gut and the brain:[4] and turn on or off multiple metabolic pathways including those for glucose, lipid, protein metabolism[5] and cell growth and survival.[6] Close to the age of "autistic regression," we add pertussis toxin, which completely disrupts G Alpha signals.[7] The opposite G proteins are on without inhibition leading to:[8]

Glycogen breakdown or gluconeogenesis. Many of these children have elevated blood sugars. There is sixty-eight percent incidence of diabetes in parents and grandparents of these children.

Lipid breakdown which increases blood fats that lead to hyperlipidemia. One-third of families has either a parent or grandparent who died from myocardial infarction at less than 55 years of age and was diagnosed with hyperlipidemia.

Cell growth differentiation and survival which leads to uncontrolled cell growth. There are 62 cases of malignancies associated with ras-oncogene in 60 families of these autistic children.[9] The measles antibody cross reacts with intermediate filaments which are the glue that hold cells together in the gut wall.[10] The loss of cell to cell connection interrupts aproptosis or the ability of neighboring cells to kill off abnormal cells. The MMR vaccine at 15 months precedes the DPT at 18 months, which turns on uncontrolled cell growth differentiation and survival.

Most families report cancer in the parents or grandparents, the most common being colon cancer.[10]The genetic defect, found in 30-50% of adult cancers, is a cancer gene (<u>ras-oncogene</u>). It is the same defect as that for congenital stationary night blindness.[11]

G protein defects cause severe loss of rod function in most autistic children.[12] They lose night vision, and light to dark shading on objects in the daylight. They sink into a "magic eye puzzle," seeing only color and shape in all of their visual field, except for a "box" in the middle, the only place they get the impression of the three dimensional nature of objects. Only when they look at television or a computer do they predictably hear the right language for what they see. They try to make sense of the world around them by lining up toys, sorting by color. They have to "see" objects by adding boxes together, thus "thinking in pictures." Their avoidance of eye contact is an attempt to get light to land off center in the retina where they have some rod function. Suddenly mothers touch feels like sandpaper on their skin. Common sounds become like nails scraped on a blackboard. We think they cannot abstract, but we are sinking these children into an abstract painting at 18 months of age and they are left trying to figure out if the language they are hearing is connected to what they are looking at, at the same time.

The defect for congenital stationary night blindness on the short arm of the X chromosome affects cell membrane calcium channels[13] which, if not functioning, block NMDA/glutamate receptors in the hippocampus,[14] where pathways connect the left and right brain with the frontal lobe. Margaret Bauman has described a lack of cell growth and differentiation in the hippocampus seen on autopsy in autistic children.[15] The frontal lobe is the seat of attention, inhibition of impulse, social judgment and all executive function.

When stimulated, these NMDA receptors, through G proteins stimulate nuclear Vitamin A receptors discovered by Ron Evans, et al Dec 1998.[16] When blocked, in the animal model, mice are unable to learn and remember changes in their environment. They act as if they have significant visual perceptual problems and have spatial learning deficits.[17]

Of concern the Hepatitis B virus protein sequence was originally isolated in the gene for a similar retinoid receptor (RAR beta),[18] which is the critical receptor important for brain plasticity and retinoid signaling in the hippocampus.[19] After the mercury is removed, I understand we will restart Hepatitis B vaccine at day one of life. Studies need to be done to determine if this plays an additive roll in the marked increase in autism.

I am using natural lipid soluble concentrated cis form of Vitamin A in cod liver oil to bypass blocked G protein pathways and turn on these central retinoid receptors. In a few days, most of these children regain eye contact and some say their "box" of clear vision grows. After two months on Vitamin A treatment some of these children, when given a single dose of bethanechol to stimulate pathways in the parasympathetic system in the gut, focus, laugh, concentrate, show a sense of humor, and talk after 30 minutes as if reconnected.[20]

This improves cognition, but they are still physically ill. When these children get the MMR vaccine, their Vitamin A stores are depleted; they can not compensate for blocked pathways. Lack of Vitamin A which has been called "the anti-infective agent," leaves them immuno-suppressed. They lack cell-mediated immunity. T cell activation, important for long term immune memory, requires 14-hydroxy retro-retinol. On cod liver oil, the only natural source of this natural substance, the children get well. The parasympathetic nervous system is blocked by the second G protein defect. These children are unable to relax, focus and digest their food. Instead, they are in sympathetic overdrive with a constant outpouring of adrenaline and stress hormones. They are anxious, pace, have dilated pupils, high blood pressure and heart rate. These and other symptoms of attention deficit hyperactivity disorder are part of this constant "fright or flight" response. These symptoms improve on bethanechol.

I live in a small middle class neighborhood with twenty-three houses. I recently counted thirty children who live in this community who are on medication for ADHD. One week ago, my oldest son who is gifted but dyslexic had twelve neighborhood friends over for dinner. As I looked around the table, all of these children, but one had dilated pupils. After two and one half months of taking vitamin A and D in cod liver oil, my son announced, "I can read now. The letters don't jump around on the page anymore." He is able to focus and his handwriting has improved dramatically. In his high school for college bound dyslexic students, 68 of 70 teenagers report seeing headlights with starbursts, a symptom of congenital stationary night blindness.

I think we are staring a disaster in the face that has affected thousands of Americans. The children with autism or dyslexia/ADHD are lucky. There are many other children not identified, just disconnected.

We must direct all of our resources and efforts to establish multidisciplinary centers to treat these children. Insurance companies should pay for evaluations, both medical and psychiatric, and treatment. These children are physically ill, immuno-suppressed with a chronic autoimmune disorder affecting multiple organ systems. Funding to look at etiology of autism, to identify children at risk prior to "autistic regression," and to prevent this disorder is imperative. Implementing vaccine policies that are safe for <u>all</u> children should become <u>our</u> first priority.

Mothers from all over the country have brought pictures of their autistic children to Washington this weekend. Most of these children were born normal and lost to "autistic regression." Look into their eyes and you will hear their silence.

Thank you

Mary N Megson, MD

End Notes

i   "Tamoxifen: Questions and Answers"
cancer.gov.
<http://www.cancer.gov/cancertopics/factsheet/therapy/tamoxifen>

ii   "HER2 Disease"
gene.com.
<http://www.gene.com/gene/products/education/oncology/
her2disease.html>

iii   "How Independent Are Vaccine Defenders?" cbsnews.com.
<http://www.cbsnews.com/stories/2008/07/25/cbsnews_
investigates/main4296175.shtml>.

iv   "Intense Therapy Improves Speech After Stroke"
webmd.com. 9 Jun 2005.
<http://www.webmd.com/stroke/news/20050609/intense-therapy-
improves-speech-after-stroke>

v   "Pervasive Developmental Disorder – Not Otherwise Specified
(PDD-NOS)" med.yale.edu.
<http://www.med.yale.edu/chldstdy/autism/pddnos.html>

vi   "Where did the idea of regrigerator mothers originate?" autism.
about.com <http://autism.about.com/od/causesofautism/p/refrig-
erator.htm>.

vii   "Generation Rescue" generationrescue.com <generationrescue.
com>.

viii   "Parent-directed, intensive early intervention for children with
pervasive developmental disorder" sciencedirect.com
< http://www.sciencedirect.com/science?_ob=ArticleURL&_

Out of the Darkness

udi=B6VDN-4118F75-5&_user=10&_rdoc=1&_
fmt=&_orig=search&_sort=d&_docanchor=&view=c&_
searchStrId=954177422&_rerunOrigin=scholar.google&_
acct=C000050221&_version=1&_urlVersion=0&_userid=10&m
d5=3756af2827eadb650730b94b8d705554 >.

ix   "Florida Diagnostic and Learning Resources System" paec.org
       <http://www.paec.org/fdlrsweb/>.

x   "House Government Reform Committee on Autism and
       Vaccines"
       vaccinationnews.com.
       <http://www.vaccinationnews.com/dailynews/june2001/megson-
       testimonycongress.htm>.

xi   "Cod Liver Oil Heath Benefits"
       homeremediesweb.com.
       <http://www.homeremediesweb.com/cod-liver-oil-health-benefits.
       php>.

xii   "Carconigenic Mercury Vapors Leach Endlessly and Profusely in
       Your Mouth." biohermit.com. 15 Aug. 2008.
       15 Aug. 2008
       <http://biohermit.wordpress.com/2008/08/15/mercury-vapors-
       leach-endlessly-and-profusely-in-your-mouth/.>

xiii   "How do people get exposed to mercury?"
       orf.od.nih.gov
       <http://orf.od.nih.gov/Environmental+Protection/Mercury+Free/
       MercuryHealthHazards.htm>.

xiv   "The GFCF Diet."
       gfcfdiet.com.
       <http://www.gfcfdiet.com/>.

xv   "Shands ranks highest among Florida hospitals." Gainesvill.Com.
       15 Jul. 2008.
       15 Jul. 2008

<http://www.gainesville.com/article/20080715/
news/272794758/1002/new&title=Shands_ranks_highest_
among_Florida_hospitals>.

xvi   "Hyperbaric Oxygen Therapy" Emedicine.Com.
        21 Jul. 2005 <http://www.emedicine.com/plastic/topic526.htm>.

xvii   "Hyperbaric Oxygen Therapy"
        Emedicine.Com.
        21 Jul. 2005
        <http://www.emedicine.com/plastic/topic526.htm>.

xviii   "Gamow"
        mild-hyperbaric-oxygen-therapy.com
        <http://www.mild-hyperbaric-oxygen-therapy.com/history-
        mild-hyperbaric-oxygen-therapy.html>

xix   "Hyperbaric Oxygen Therapy Testimonials"
        whitakerwellness.com.
        <http://whitakerwellness.com/testimonials/hyperbaric_oxygen_
        therapy/?>.

xx   "The Effects of Hyperbaric Oxygen Therapy on Oxidative Stress,
        inflammation, and Symptoms in children with Autism: an open-
        label pilot study"
        ibiomedcentral.com.
        <http://www.biomedcentral.com/1471-2431/7/36>.

xxi   "Hyperbaric oxygen therapy for the adjunctive treatment of
        traumatic brain injury"
        Cochrane.org
        <http://www.cochrane.org/reviews/en/ab004609.html>.

xxii   "Conditions Treated with Hyperbaric Therapy."
        HBOTreatment.Com.
        <http://www.hbotreatment.com/
        conditions.htm

xxiii "Complications and Side Effects of Hyperbaric Oxygen Therapy"
ncbi.nlm.nih.gov.
Feb. 2001
<http://www.ncbi.nlm.nih.gov/pubmed/10685584>.

xxiv "The Stem Cell Debate"
lifeissues.net.
<http://www.lifeissues.net/writers/edi/edi_06stemcelldebate.
html>.

xxv "Monitoring Stem Cell Research" bioethics.gov. Jan. 2004.
Jan. 2004
<http://www.bioethics.gov/reports/stemcell/glossary.html>.

xxvi "Ukraine Babies in Stem Cell Probe"
news.bbc.co.uk.
12 Dec. 2006.
12 Dec. 2006 <http://news.bbc.co.uk/2/hi/europe/6171083.stm>.

xxvii "Family Research Council: Adult Stem Cell Success Stories 2008"
frc.org.
<http://www.frc.org/insight/adult-stem-cell-sucess-stories-2008-
jan-june>.

xxviii "Advances and Best Practices in Autism, Learning Disabilities
ADHD." Thehelpgroup.com.
26 Sep. 2008.
< http://www.thehelpgroup.com/pdf/SUMMIT_08_WEB_
Brochure.pdf>.

xxix "Doctors Use Bone Marrow Stem Cells to Repair a Heart"
query.nytimes.com. 10 Oct. 2008.
10 Oct. 2008
<http://query.nytimes.com/gst/fullpage.html?res=9B06E7D6133
FF934A35750C0A9659C8B63>.

xxx   "Stem Cells and Tissue Regeneration" nature.com. 2003.
2003
\<http://www.nature.com/bmt/journal/v32/n1s/full/1703939a.
html\>.

xxxi   "Stem Cell Therapy for Autism" translational-medicine.Com.
27 Jul. 2007
\<http://www.translational-medicine.com/content/pdf/1479-5876-
5-30.pdf\>.

xxxii   "Treating Crohn's Disease with Hematopoietic Stem Cell
Transplantation" <u>surgicalroundsonline.com</u>
Mar. 2008
\<http://www.surgicalroundsonline.com/issues/articles/2008-
03_04.asp\>.

xxxiii   "Effect of hyperbaric stress on yeast morphology: study by auto-
mated image analysis"
http://cat.inist.fr.
\<http://cat.inist.fr/?aModele=afficheN&cpsidt=16439413\>

xxxiv   "Coloidial Silver"
http://www.medicinebeeherbals.com
http://www.medicinebeeherbals.com/article-colloidal-silver.php

xxxv   "The Rediscovery of a Super Antibiotic?" dazer.com
\<http://www.dazer.com/silver-1.html.\>

xxxvi   "Historic Perspectives on Clinical Use and Efficacy of Silver"
http://www.hydrosolinfo.com
http://www.hydrosolinfo.com/articles/history-of-silver.php

xxxvii   "Colloidal Silver – the Antibiotic Alternative" altmedicineshop.com
\<http://www.altmedicineshop.com/ProductInfo/Collodialsilver.
htm\>.

xxxviii "Real-life 'Blue Guy' shrugs off his skin color"
msnbc.msn.com
<http://www.msnbc.msn.com/id/22536241/>

xxxix "Bacterial Endotoxins/Pyrogens"
fda.gov
<http://www.fda.gov/ICECI/Inspections/InspectionGuides/Inspec-
tionTechnicalGuides/ucm072918.htm >

xl "The History of Gold"
<http://www.crucible.org/gold_colloids.htm>.

xli "Gold Nanoparticles 101" nanogloss.com
<http://nanogloss.com/nanoparticles/gold-nanoparticles-101/>.

xlii "Alchemists Workshop" alchemistsworkshop.com
<http://alchemistsworkshop.com/_wsn/page12.html>.

xliii "Mind Alive Inc."
http://www.mindalive.ca.
<http://www.mindalive.ca/2_2_5.htm>

xliv "Alpha-Stim Cranial Electrical Stimulation"
< http://alpha-stim.com>.

xlv "Modulation of osteogenesis in human mesenchymal stem cells
by specific pulsed electromagnetic field stimulation" interscience.
wiley.com
<http://www3.interscience.wiley.com/journal/122249176/
abstract?CRETRY=1&SRETRY=0>.

Made in the USA
Columbia, SC
04 July 2023

19462373R00096